Betty Shine was born in Kennington in 1929. Her grandmother was a spiritualist. Before she became a practising healer, she was a professional singer, and she has at times taught vitamin and mineral therapy, hand analysis and yoga. She lives and practises in the south of England. Her other three books, *Mind to Mind*, *Mind Magic* and *Betty Shine's Mind Workbook* are all available in Corgi.

Also by Betty Shine

**MIND TO MIND
MIND MAGIC
BETTY SHINE'S MIND WORKBOOK**

and published by Corgi Books

BETTY SHINE

The ultimate energy that could change the world

MIND WAVES

CORGI BOOKS

MIND WAVES
A CORGI BOOK : 0 552 13998 X

Originally published in Great Britain by Bantam Press,
a division of Transworld Publishers Ltd

PRINTING HISTORY
Bantam Press edition published 1993
Corgi edition published 1994
Corgi edition reprinted 1995

Set in 10/12pt Linotype Plantin by
County Typesetters, Margate, Kent

Corgi Books are published by Transworld Publishers Ltd,
61–63 Uxbridge Road, Ealing, London W5 5SA,
in Australia by Transworld Publishers (Australia) Pty Ltd,
15–25 Helles Avenue, Moorebank, NSW 2170,
and in New Zealand by Transworld Publishers (NZ) Ltd,
3 William Pickering Drive, Albany, Auckland.

Reproduced, printed and bound in Great Britain by
Cox & Wyman Ltd, Reading, Berks.

This book is dedicated to the children of the world,
in the hope that they may learn to use
their psychic powers to transform this planet

My love to Julia and Mark Smith
for their encouragement

Contents

Introduction

Since I published my first book, *Mind to Mind*, my life has changed beyond all recognition.

The letters I have received from all over the world have been extremely encouraging, and have given me strength. I have also been showered with love from strangers. I thank those people from the bottom of my heart.

The publication of my second book, *Mind Magic*, brought an even greater response. I tried to give my readers the knowledge they had asked for, and also the ability to prove themselves through the exercises therein. It is quite apparent from the letters I receive that *Mind Magic* has opened many doors, and there are now healing groups all around the world successfully using these exercises.

This book, *Mind Waves*, completes the psychic course. It gives simple answers to the whole structure of the paranormal and is a must for any budding psychic.

It is also the last of the *Mind* books.

I do not write books and forget them. I read them again frequently, because no matter who we are, we do tend to forget psychic laws.

For those of you who own all three books, let me remind you that every word and every page carries healing energy. For no matter how many times a book is reprinted, the soul of the author is in it for ever.

I hope that my books will give healing, peace and happiness to everyone who comes into contact with them.

It may only be a brief encounter, but it will change your life.

As you read on, it will become clear to you that mind waves control not only our private lives, but the world as a whole.

Individual mind waves linking with like minds become an ocean, and unless the waves are positive we could all lose everything to a mass of negative energy.

I believe that this book will bring greater understanding to all who read it.

PART ONE

TELEPATHY

1

A Boy Called Alex

> If I have put into my book anything which can fill the young mind with better thoughts of death, or soften the grief of older hearts; If I have written one word which can afford pleasure or consolation to old or young in time of trial, I shall consider it as something achieved – something which I shall be glad to look back upon in afterlife.
>
> Charles Dickens, *The Old Curiosity Shop*.

I usually spend two hours every morning reading the hundreds of letters that are delivered to my home weekly. On one particular morning my hand was guided to a letter that sat amidst a huge pile. I opened it, and began to read. The letter was from a lady called Felicity whose son Alex, once an extremely intelligent and healthy boy, had been struck down with the brain virus, subacute sclerosing panencephalitis. According to the doctor's prognosis, the virus would cause severe brain damage, and Alex was not expected to live beyond three months to a year, indeed, his health was deteriorating every day.

When I had finished reading all the other letters, I decided to go into my healing room and ask for guidance. My workload over the past year had been increasing and I was feeling tired. If I accepted Alex I would have to be dedicated and I wasn't sure that I would have the time. On the other hand, I do like a challenge. Healing works in mysterious ways, surprising me all the time. The question was, would I be able to dedicate myself to one boy when so many others needed my help?

I had been meditating for about ten minutes when I was given the instruction to contact Alex telepathically. His mother had mentioned in her letter the name of the hospital in London where he was, so I closed my eyes and reached out to him.

Within seconds I found myself listening to a story about Alex's goldfish, and about how upset he had been when they were killed!

'Who on earth would kill a child's goldfish?' I wondered.

I decided that it was time to speak to Alex's mother, Felicity. I wanted her to confirm his story; if it was true, I would know that I could communicate with him even though he was in a coma-like state and that I should accept him as a patient.

When his mother answered the phone, I introduced myself, told her what I had learnt from Alex and asked if she could confirm it. Her immediate response was to wonder why he was talking about goldfish at a time like this. The fact that I had had a telepathic conversation with someone who was not only fifty miles away from me, but who was unable to speak, seemed to have completely passed her by! I asked again whether she could confirm the story. 'Yes, it is true,' she said, and told me what had happened.

Apparently, the fishtank had needed sterilizing, and after temporarily placing the goldfish in a bowl, she had poured boiling water into the fishtank. Enter Alex's father, Jeremy. He saw the goldfish in the small bowl, felt sorry for them and popped them back into the fishtank –

and into the boiling water. Needless to say, the whole family were terribly upset by this, and Jeremy, of course, was in the doghouse.

After Felicity had told me this story, she asked again why Alex should be so concerned about his pets when his own life was in danger. I explained that when someone is very seriously ill or in a coma-like state, the mind energy is about 95 per cent out of the body. In that state, Alex would be linking with other minds, and would know that I needed to have information that could be confirmed.

I promised her that I would give Alex absent healing immediately, and then every day at 9 a.m., 12 midday and 9 p.m. I asked her to let me know when Alex was able to travel so that I could arrange an appointment for him.

My first absent healing session with Alex was quiet and uneventful, and yet there was something special about it which I couldn't explain.

Felicity rang me the following day to say that Alex's tummy had rumbled quite loudly at the time I was giving him the absent healing. She was thrilled, as she had read in my first book *Mind to Mind* that this often happened when someone received contact healing. It had given her a glimmer of hope when she needed it most.

The day of Alex's first appointment with me arrived. His parents collected him from hospital and brought him by car.

My first sight of Alex filled me with compassion – a child with unseeing eyes, a nasogastric tube, and lungs so congested that he could hardly breathe.

They laid him on the healing couch, and made him as comfortable as possible. Then a suction tube was placed in his mouth to remove mucus from his throat and lungs.

I placed my hands on his head and closed my eyes.

Clairvoyantly, I could 'see' the congestion in the throat and lungs, and knew that healing would be extremely difficult if this was not removed. I decided to give him a psychic operation to remove the congestion and I explained to his parents what I was about to do in case they had any objection. They hadn't.

I mentally placed energy tubes through Alex's body into his lungs, and I was about to attach pumps when spirit hands appeared and asked me to put my own hands aside. They were speaking about my energy hands of course, as my physical hands were nowhere near Alex. They obviously thought that they could make a better job of it.

I described what was taking place to his parents. Whether they believed me or not would depend on the results.

I watched whilst two pairs of spirit hands inserted tubes and attached two pumps. Then the mucus was pumped out of Alex's lungs. After a few minutes, the difference in him was miraculous. The terrible rasping sound had gone, and he was breathing quietly and peacefully.

Felicity was the first to speak. 'I can't believe what I have just seen,' she said. Jeremy couldn't believe it either, and they both sat there, just staring at Alex.

I continued with hands-on healing for about an hour. By the time they left, Alex was breathing quietly and was at peace.

This spirit operation had been extraordinary in many ways. Apparently, Alex's temperature had been around 103° from the time he had been ill, and although it had started to drop after the first session of absent healing, it returned to normal after the spirit operation. His congested lungs and high temperature had been a major source of anxiety, and the doctors had said that a chest infection would be Alex's worst enemy. But after his first visit to me, the suction machine was not needed again unless he was sick in the car.

Appointments were made for Alex to have healing sessions with me and absent healing was being given every day. It was during the absent healing and contact sessions that Alex and I had telepathic conversations. He used to describe his hospital room and the nurses that tended him. He was especially vehement about the nurses he didn't like. He was particularly pleased that he was able to convey messages through myself to his parents, and that these messages were being confirmed.

During one of his visits, he showed me telepathic pictures of a box with drawers in, in which he had kept his stamps. Julia, his nanny, was present at the time. She told me that the information was correct, and that the box was blue. She added, 'In hospital he has Capital Gold on the radio, and they are advertising a new set of stamps for collectors.' She laughed. 'I think he is giving me a hint – I always buy him new stamps when they come out.'

On another occasion, Alex told me how annoyed he used to be when Julia wouldn't allow him to go with his skateboard beyond the square where he lived. Apparently, she thought it was too dangerous. This was confirmed by Julia.

During one of their earlier visits, I had had a message from a close relation of the family called Harry. From all accounts he was an extremely aggressive and strong character when he was alive, and from his tone he had not changed at all. When he had finished giving survival evidence he said that he was organizing everything – presumbly he meant everything connected with Alex's healing.

Of course, this was a very exciting time for everyone concerned, but especially for Jeremy. He had only agreed to attend the healing sessions to keep Felicity company; he did not believe in healing and had, up to that point, been an agnostic. However, events were overwhelming him and he gradually had a complete change of heart. After all, when he had seen his son so seriously ill that he could not communicate at all, and then listened to telepathic communications from him and seen him relieved of serious problems, what else could Jeremy do?

There was one occasion at a healing session when Jeremy was telling me that they were thinking of having him home for good. Alex linked with me and said, 'Tell him that if he cleans the space at the back of the stairs there will be just enough room for a single bed. After all, there is only an old bureau and a lot of old books there. Also, they won't have the problem of carrying me upstairs all the time.' Jeremy looked dumbstruck and then he laughed. 'Betty, that is absolutely true. I can't believe this.'

I must confess I was finding it all quite incredible myself.

By this time I was communicating with Alex on a day-to-day basis. When Felicity telephoned, I passed on the messages from her son which I had received whilst giving him absent healing and they were always confirmed. Sometimes there were requests from him, and these she also understood.

Julia was reduced to tears once when Alex linked with me during contact healing and said that he wanted to give a message to his sister who was at home. He thanked her for everything she had done for him since his illness, especially as he had felt that she had always thought of him as a pest before he was sick. Again, this was confirmed – although what elder sister hasn't thought like that about a younger brother. However, she had dedicated a large proportion of her time to Alex when he was in hospital.

One week, Alex arrived with a swollen knee, and was in a lot of pain. I placed my hand over his knee, and could feel the swelling reducing rapidly. Jeremy saw the outline of the swelling, and both he and Julia were amazed at how quickly it disappeared. Julia told me afterwards that she was completely flabbergasted.

Alex was also beginning to respond in small ways. On one occasion I asked him out loud to try to lift his left leg. A few seconds passed and then the leg began to move slightly and he managed to lift his leg off the couch. I repeated the request, but this time for his right leg. And the right leg lifted off the couch.

These were exciting days, and helped to keep Alex's parents' hopes high when there had seemed to be no hope at all. It was also very stimulating for me. Something quite extraordinary was going on.

One day, Alex's parents were accompanied by a friend. During the healing session, Alex linked in with me and told me that he would like a cat. The friend said, 'I have three cats – ask him which one he would like.' Alex replied that he would like the tortoiseshell cat. The friend told us that the cat was blind, and I said that I thought Alex had chosen the tortoiseshell because of its handicap. There would obviously be an affinity between them. 'Perhaps you would like to bring the cat for healing on Alex's next appointment?' I suggested.

Felicity told me that the previous day her friend had discussed taking one of her cats to visit Alex. She had thought it would be company for him. It was quite obvious that he was aware of everything that was going on around him, and wanted to tell us so. By repeating these conversations telepathically, he could do this.

Alex's parents brought the cat to Alex's next healing

session and after he had received his healing, they took the cat out of her basket. She was beautiful, but her eyes moved rapidly all the time. I placed my hands over her eyes and when I removed them ten minutes later the movement had slowed down quite considerably. She was put back in her basket, and they left.

The next day, Felicity phoned to say that the cat was able to see, and where before it had just lain quietly on Alex's bed, it was now going outside for the first time, climbing trees and generally having great fun.

The cat came along with Alex several times, and the difference in the animal was amazing. The eye movement was slowing down all the time, and the cat was obviously very pleased with herself. Apparently she had been a feral cat, and had been in a very bad way when the friend found her as a kitten and decided to look after her.

Something quite extraordinary was also happening to Jeremy. At each weekly session, he was given detailed survival evidence, sometimes from people he had not thought about for years. On one occasion, before giving Alex trance healing, I asked Jeremy to look at me during the healing. I must admit, I did not know why I asked him to do this. However, he obeyed. When I came out of trance, he was as white as a sheet. I asked him if there was anything wrong. His answer was, 'Sorry, I must have a cigarette,' and with that he walked out into the garden. I talked to Alex for a while until his father came back inside. I asked him if he had seen anything whilst I was healing Alex. He didn't say a word, just sat down and closed his eyes. After a few minutes he said, 'I have a scientific mind, Betty, and I cannot believe what I saw in this room.' After much coaxing he told me about it.

'When you went into trance and started healing Alex, I saw a bright yellow light all around you and Alex. After a few minutes it changed to blue. Then a Red Indian gradually manifested in your place.' He described the Indian in detail. 'He had black straight hair parted in the middle, a strong face and aquiline nose. A very powerful individual. I was not frightened at the time, but when he disappeared and I saw you again I was shaken because the light was still there. I looked away and then back again, but there it was. That's why I went out into the garden. I am still shaking,' he said, holding out his hands for me to see.

Julia then gave me her version of what had happened. 'I shall never forget today,' she said. 'He kept saying to me, "Can you see it, can you see it?" He made me move all around the room whilst you were giving healing, but I couldn't see anything at all. He was desperate for me to see the light. I suppose he wanted to reassure himself that he wasn't going mad.' She went on, 'He even left the room at one time and came back rubbing his eyes, trying to recover his composure. I must admit I felt rather jealous.'

She later told me that on their way home Jeremy had said that he would have to re-evaluate his whole way of thinking on life and death. She found this astonishing considering that he was such an agnostic. He then told her that he had been feeling apprehensive about his visit to me that day because of what had happened a week earlier. He had apparently seen the light, and had seen a small female figure holding a candle behind my shoulder. It was later established that this was a friend's daughter. I had told him that the little girl had not given a name but had shown me the letter T. Neither he nor Julia could shed any light on this until they discussed it with Felicity on their return home. She linked it up immediately. The girl's surname began with T.

The Red Indian seen by Jeremy confirmed something that Michael Bentine had told me. One day, when I was giving him healing at his home, he waited for me to finish, then said, 'Betty, whilst you were healing me a very powerful Indian manifested in your place. I think that is why I am impelled to bring you back gifts from the reservations.' Indeed, Michael has brought me several gifts, one of which is a sand picture of an Indian healing ceremony, and which has very powerful vibrations. Even people who do not know what it is remark on the energy emanating from it. I must admit though, at the time I laughed and pulled his leg about the so-called manifestation. But he looked at me and said, 'You will have confirmation of this.' He was very positive, but on the way home I said to Alan, 'Fancy Michael coming out with that story about a Red Indian.' I am afraid I dismissed it from my mind.

After Jeremy had left, I called Michael and told him what had happened. I also told him I had not really believed him when he had given me the same story, and I apologized. Michael laughed, and said, 'I told you it would be confirmed and I am so pleased that it has been. More so, that it should come from someone who has no understanding of these things. That makes it even more exciting – and what a wonderful experience for him.' I told him that the poor man had been very badly shaken. He laughed. 'I must admit when you see someone manifest for the first time it is a bit frightening, especially when you are not expecting it.'

During another healing session, Alex repeatedly gave me a name that no-one recognized. I felt a bit concerned, because he was making such an effort to tell me something and I seemed to be letting him down. It wasn't until several months later that Felicity was able to tell me that the name Alex had given me was that of a young girl, related to the family by marriage, who had just been killed in a car crash. Alex was obviously trying to warn us.

Here was a young boy, completely immobilized and unable to speak or move his eyes, and yet capable of superb telepathic transmissions – and in the case of the warning, giving clairvoyance.

On another occasion Alex asked me to persuade his father not to smoke in the car as it made him feel sick. Apparently, Julia had also asked Jeremy not to smoke in the car as she was aware that it was making Alex feel ill, but her request did not have the same impact as a direct one from Alex: his father stopped smoking in the car from that time. Poor Dad, I felt that he was getting quite a raw deal, but he stood up to all the lectures and the amazing phenomena quite well. There had been a noticeable difference in his personality since he had begun attending the healing with Alex. He was more peaceful, and as he sat on the couch during the sessions, he too received healing and was cured of various ailments that he had not mentioned to me.

Alex was also allowing his personality to shine through the telepathic communications. Once when Julia brushed his hair forward, he said, 'Don't do that.' When I repeated this to her, she told me he had always said that when she brushed his hair in that way. On another occasion I was asking him to lift his arms and legs and without realizing it had slightly raised my voice. His immediate reaction was to tell me not to shout.

At the time of writing this book I have given clair- voyance, survival evidence and telepathic communciations for eighteen months to everyone who has accompanied Alex, and all of it has been substantiated. But his father has received the most information. Nearly every time Jeremy arrives, there is someone waiting to speak to him.

Why? Because he has to look after Alex during the day, and he needs the strength and hope to carry on. People in other dimensions do not waste their time giving regular evidence except in the case of great need. Jeremy was given the evidence, energy and help he needed.

Spirit doctors were always with us from the very first contact healing I gave Alex. They repeatedly looked into his eyes and at his head, and on one occasion they told me that they were putting an energy field around his brain so that it would be protected. From that time, he has used his eyes far more than he had previously.

Felicity has also become attuned to Alex during the night. She told me, 'I wake frequently to find that Alex has slipped forward and is uncomfortable. One night, after you had asked him to lift his arm during healing, I woke to find that he was repeatedly lifting his arm. He obviously wanted to show me his efforts and had communicated with me telepathically. I also often wake up to see him looking at me, obviously needing comfort.' This is a typical mind-to-mind contact.

It was whilst I was giving him healing in the summer that he told me how much he missed having strawberries. Apparently, he loved the fresh strawberries they had for tea when they visited the family cottage in the country. He described the cottage and surroundings accurately.

On another occasion, he gave me a description of the building where he went swimming, guiding me through the doors and down corridors until we reached the bath itself. The picture he created was so clear.

A later appointment found Alex giving his father a lecture for not loving the cat as much as he should. He said that his father was annoyed that the cat had freedom while Alex had not. Alex said that he was thrilled the cat had its freedom now that it had recovered its sight, that he still

26

loved to have it around, as he could hear it and it comforted him. His father was astounded.

This was not the first lecture Jeremy had received from Alex, but I think it shook him the most. He admitted to me that they had only borrowed the cat because it liked to sleep on Alex's bed all the time, but after its blindness had been cured, it behaved like a normal cat, climbing around in the garden and in the home, anywhere but on Alex's bed. He said, 'I have been thinking lately that it is just a freeloader.' I laughed. 'Will you try something for me?' I asked, and he said that he would. 'Go back home and start loving the cat. If you do this, he will spend time on Alex's bed again.' Jeremy smiled. 'OK, it's a deal.' On their next visit, he told me that he had been treating the cat very well, and that it was now spending more time on the bed with Alex.

There are so many wonderful stories that I could tell you about Alex, his family and his friends. The latest is that he complains bitterly to me when he doesn't receive his quota of jellies. Jeremy has become so nervous that if he hasn't given Alex jelly during the week, he makes sure that he has it the night before he visits me.

Alex also told me that someone had brought a dog to see him. I turned to Julia and said, 'Alex really enjoyed having that little dog around the other night. He is telling me what a lovely atmosphere it created.' Julia told me that three nights before our appointment, she had taken Pickle, a Norfolk terrier, to see Alex. Before that he had not seen any other animals except the cat during the past eighteen months. Once again Julia was amazed at Alex's telepathic abilities.

The eighteen months since my first telepathic communication with Alex have been incredible, not just for me but for everyone who has been connected with him and who has witnessed the communication I have had with him. The telepathic communication goes on, as well as the survival evidence. It seems that it will never end and we do not wish it to.

I believe that Alex was chosen to prove to the world that the mind can still communcate even though the physical body is unable to function. It is a major breakthrough, brought about by minds in other dimensions. No longer should family and friends grieve because they cannot speak to someone in this condition. They can, and they will be understood, even if they never receive a reply. The mind cannot be destroyed. It is for ever. When the physical body dies, the mind goes on to other dimensions. The survival evidence I have received leaves me in no doubt about this.

I would like to put your mind at rest should you ever have to make the decision to turn off a life support machine. When you are asked to make this decision, you will be left alone to think about it quietly. During that time your mind will be linking with that of the patient. Mind waves will go back and forth between you and the patient and when it comes to making a decision, you will automatically have picked up the patient's wishes.

Although Alex is a child, he makes a tremendous impact upon me when he wishes to convey a message. In fact, there is no way I can ignore him when he wishes to communicate. He has given pleasure to everyone around him, but most of all he has taught us so much that we will never forget. He has taught us to love, to believe, and he has given me a story that I can tell the world. Hopefully, it will make an impact and help to change our society into a more caring one. Most of all, Alex has taught us to have respect for people who are immobile; although they cannot move or express themselves, their minds are still very much intact and aware.

Alex is progressing all the time. He moves his eyes, following people around the room. He can make a fuss by changing his breathing audibly if he does not like something.

At the beginning of 1990, Alex told me that he could see himself standing in nine months time. This seemed to be an impossibility. In August, during one of his physiotherapy sessions, Alex was put into a standing position on a tilt table. He loved it, and yes, the clairvoyance he gave himself came true. He still loves to be in that position.

We all have great hopes for his future. Hope is power, and we must never lose it for we cannot let Alex down when he himself has achieved so much.

In the next chapter I will explain how I was taught to give the kind of psychic surgery that I have mentioned in this chapter.

2

Psychic Surgery

In the previous chapter, I described an operation that was performed on Alex, the first part being carried out by myself and the second by spirit doctors. Although, in my previous books, I have mentioned psychic operations I have never before given details of how I was taught in the first place.

In this chapter I would like to take you step-by-step through the learning process of those first two years. I think you will find it as intriguing as I did.

Although the medium Charles Horrey, who was mentioned in *Mind to Mind*, told me that a surgeon was making it clear to him that he wanted to work through me, and indeed, gave me his name, nothing on this earth could have prepared me for the actual experience. As you read on, you will understand why.

Psychic surgery may sound alarming, but the method I use is perfectly safe, and over the last eighteen years I have had no complaints. In fact, every operation brings relief and very often miraculous cures.

The minds of many surgeons use me as a channel, and I feel privileged that they should do so. Their transmissions are an example of mind waves at their best. However, I must confess, I did not welcome them with open arms.

I was told by my spirit friends that surgeons were eager to help with the healing I was doing – which corroborated the information given to me by Charles Horrey. I thought this was all very dramatic, but I was still not prepared for the tutoring I was to receive over the next few years.

Psychic surgery is carried out on the energy counterpart. Those of you who have read *Mind to Mind* and *Mind Magic* will be familiar with this term. However, let me explain. All life is energy, and the energy counterpart fits neatly into the physical system, mirroring it on the non-physical plane. The aura – a word much used but little understood – is an extension of the counterpart. It protrudes about an inch and a half all around the physical body when the latter is healthy, and virtually disappears when it is not. The ability to 'see' this energy is a gift bestowed upon me.

Through telepathic communication from another dimension I have been taught how to make my own instruments and perform psychic surgery – with my mind.

How did it begin? About two years after I became a professional healer, I was sitting quietly with my eyes closed, giving healing to a patient, when I saw a mind picture of a scalpel. Before I had time to study it closely, it disappeared. What happened next was quite remarkable. I saw a small cloud of energy, and as I studied it, a scalpel was being formed out of the energy. The scene then shifted and I saw spirit hands cut into the energy counterpart of my patient's stomach. The energy counterpart opened up, and the hands pulled out a substance that was reminiscent of cottonwool balls. When the last ball had been removed, I saw a spirit finger being drawn along the opening – and the energy counterpart was again normal.

To say that I was amazed would certainly be an understatement. I looked at my patient, who seemed to be in a state of trance. I sat beside her for about ten minutes trying to collect my thoughts, having just witnessed something that was quite incredible. If healing was to be aided in this way, it would certainly speed the recovery rate.

My patient opened her eyes. I held her hand, and asked how she felt. She smiled. 'I feel as though I have been a long way away.' She tried to sit up, but promptly lay down again. 'I also feel as if I've been drinking!' I smiled and explained that healing could make you feel like that. I helped her to sit up, and she carefully put her feet to the ground. She was a bit shaky, so I guided her to a chair. As she sat down I asked whether she had felt any pain whilst I had been giving her healing. 'No, I didn't feel anything at all,' she replied, 'but I did visit this incredible place – it was so peaceful I didn't want to return. Where do you think I was?' 'I think it was your special place,' I replied. 'We all have a special place that we visit when we are asleep. Healing releases the mind energy, which in turn can travel beyond this dimension. Now that you are aware of this place you will only have to think of it and you will be there. You have been given a very special gift today.' I looked at the joy on her face. 'Healing opens many doors, and curing an illness is a very small part of the whole. One day you will know more.' She was delighted with her experience, and made another appointment for the following week.

I had decided not to speak to her about the spirit operation at that point. I knew so little myself and thought it would be more appropriate to wait and see what the future held.

As it happened, I did not have to wait very long. The next morning I had a telephone call from the same patient saying that she had noticed a red scar on her stomach whilst dressing. It was about four inches long. To put her mind at rest, I decided to tell her what had happened. I explained that the experience was new to me, but that did not seem to worry her at all. 'I believe that if the spirit world is in control, then I am in safe hands,' she said and seemed quite delighted by it all. I asked her to keep me informed of any further events. She promised to do this, and called me the following day to tell me that the scar had disappeared and that she was feeling very well.

When she arrived for her next healing session, her face was a picture which told its own story. The chronic bowel problems she had been suffering with for years had gone. She was absolutely delighted. 'Whoever carried out the operation on me has done a super job,' she said. 'The only sad thing is that I don't need you any more, and I so enjoyed the visits.' I gave her healing and she left. I did not see her again but she sent me a Christmas card every year for the next five years.

A few days later, whilst healing, I saw an instrument appear again. It disappeared, as before, and was again followed by a cloud of energy. An instrument materialized. There was no doubt at all that someone was trying to teach me how to make my own surgical instruments with my mind. The now familiar procedure followed. The scalpel, held by the spirit hands, cut into the energy counterpart, which opened up, exposing thin ropes of substance. What was it? Almost as soon as I asked the unspoken question, I knew it was energy – a useless energy. Then I had a mind picture of ectoplasm, the life-force that leaves the physical body of a medium when in trance. This substance looks very much like muslin, and covers a spirit person so that they can be seen. When it leaves, that same spirit person is once again invisible to most people. It seemed to me that this same force that gives life could also take it away if it becomes a dead-force. This was becoming more fascinating by the hour.

I was still in a dilemma. How was I going to make the instruments with my mind? It was all very well to show me these things but how could I actually do it? And another point, how could I manufacture energy hands? More important still, how would I know what to do, and to which patient? The unanswered questions were tumbling about in my mind.

This latest operation was being carried out on a lady who suffered with gallstones. The cut had been quite small, about one inch. I decided not to tell her about the operation: it was important for my records that I did not induce a psychosomatic response. However, she later remarked that she had felt extremely hot, and that her body had tingled all over during the healing.

She telephoned the next day to say that a multi-coloured bruise had appeared on her stomach. It was not very big, about one and a half inches. I described the operation that I had seen being performed on her the previous day, and she was delighted and hoped that she had been cured. I told her that it would be better to wait and see, but I felt very optimistic.

She called the following day to say that the bruise had disappeared overnight. She told me that she had a hospital appointment in seven days and that she would report back to me. After the appointment, she informed me that the specialist could find no sign of the gallstones at all – she had insisted on tests – and had given all sorts of excuses as to why they were not there. When she told him about the healing, he just dismissed it. Well, that was nothing unusual; my patients nearly always have the same response from the medical profession. Although the doctors themselves cannot find an answer, the majority will not accept that other types of non-medical healing can work.

When I had time, I sat down and thought about the new

phenomenon that had entered my life. I was not at all sure that I wanted the responsibility – in fact it was terrifying. How was I supposed to imitate the spirit action? If I found the answer, could I injure someone in the process? I decided I did not need this hassle in my life, and I was determined to block it out next time. Surely my mind was powerful enough to counteract what was happening to me?

A week passed, and the healing sessions were normal, happy and successful. Who needed psychic surgery? Two days later, I knew I should not have thought that way. It all started again – perhaps there was a frustrated surgeon who was bored with his afterlife.

This time I was healing a male patient with a serious back problem. Although his back had responded to ordinary healing, the recovery was slow. As I was sitting quietly with my hands on his spine, I saw an instrument, slightly smaller than the scalpel I had seen in previous operations. My heart sank. I had been using the power of my mind to blot it out, and it was not working. The familiar sequences continued. Obviously, a mind far more powerful than my own was at work. I could not ignore it. A cut was made halfway down the spine, and the energy body opened. Fingers drew out gossamer filaments of energy, and when the final pieces had been withdrawn a finger sealed the cut.

Again the patient was very sleepy, and I sat by his side until he opened his eyes. I asked him to get off the couch and stand up, and he did. 'That's funny,' he said, a quizzical look on his face. 'My back feels as if I've had a deadening agent injected into it.' 'Perhaps you have,' I replied, smiling. 'One never knows what really goes on whilst healing is taking place. All sorts of miraculous things can happen.'

It surprised me that he did not call me the following day – I was so sure that he would have seen bruising or a scar.

On his next visit he told me that a burn had appeared on his back after the previous session. I told him about the operation, and he could not believe it. He told me that he had had no pain since he last saw me. 'It has been the most incredible week,' he said. 'I feel as though I have been reborn. What did the spirit person do to me?' I described the operation procedure to him, and told him that I thought the substance that had been removed was some sort of dead or negative energy. I explained that I could not tell him very much as I was only a spectator at the moment.

A few days later, I was sitting meditating in my healing room when a dominant male spirit voice spoke to me. He told me to listen very carefully as he was going to teach me how to create my own instruments. He said that I was an ideal subject because of the quality of my mind.

The lessons were illuminating. First of all, he told me about energy, particularly life-force. I had apparently been correct in my assumption that the substance removed from the body was negative life-force, trapped in a blockage and ineffective within the energy system – which had, literally, become screwed up. Hence the balls, ropes and threads that I had seen. Until these were removed, a successful healing could not take place. Apparently the shape of the energy had no special significance, and was only due to the type of blockage that had occurred. I was also informed that most diseases are caused by negative energy blockages and that the circuit must be cleared at all times.

The second lesson was to teach me how, with visualization, I could create instruments from the energy cloud that

36

was presented to me. I practised this art with the spirit for about ten minutes until I was fairly proficient. It was not as difficult as I had thought it would be.

The third lesson was an actual operation. He taught me how to take the instrument with my mind, and, by visualizing my own hands in energy, I could cut through the body's energy counterpart.

The last lesson was how to remove the negative energy and seal the cut. I was taught how to remove everything that seemed to be interfering with the correct functioning of the system, and, no matter how long it took, to wait for the last tiny pieces to be eased away. This piece of information was far more important than I realized at the time. The cut, I was told, would simply disappear if I drew my finger along it.

When I asked questions, I was told to take one thing at a time. It seemed that I had been chosen to receive this gift whether I wanted it or not. Apparently, I was going to give my solo performance the next day.

Needless to say, I did not sleep much that night.

The following day, I had about twelve appointments. I had no idea who was going to be on the receiving end of my energy knife.

The first three patients came and went after normal healing. The fourth was a man with a crippled knee, for which the doctors had been unable to give a diagnosis. He was lying on the couch, and I had my eyes closed with my hands on his knee, when an instrument appeared and was gone in a second. Then the cloud appeared. At this point I visualized the instrument, as instructed, and it gradually reappeared. It was a much slower process than when the spirit surgeon had re-formed it, but it worked. Just as I was wondering what I was going to do with it, a small light appeared over the kneecap. This was obviously where I was supposed to cut. Again, as instructed by my teacher, I mentally visualized my own hands taking the scalpel, and made a cut in the knee cap. The energy body opened and balls of energy were revealed. I was told to remove them, and they de-materialized as I did so.

My patient was asleep when the operation was finished. When he woke up about five minutes later, he sat up and swung his legs round to stand on the floor, a little gingerly at first. Then he laughed, 'I can't believe this,' he said. 'Look at me.'

He was crouching and standing, flexing his knee. I decided to tell him about the operation, but I'm afraid I did not tell him it was my first. He left absolutely delighted with the result.

I was thrilled. There was obviously a lot to learn, but now I had faith in my spirit teacher and myself. I realized that I had been given the simplest of problems, and that more difficult cases lay ahead.

I performed many spirit operations over the next six months, all successful. Although, I did make the mistake of being too impatient whilst removing energy during one operation, and I did not wait until every little piece had been removed. Consequently, I had to repeat the process later, so wasting much time. I soon learned that one could not ignore even the smallest detail.

It was being made clear to me in messages and by actions that the body cannot heal itself if negative energy has built up to such a degree that it is causing pressure on a major organ, or indeed, anywhere in the body.

The important meridian lines are energy tubes which conduct life-force around the body. If one or more are blocked at any point, the life-force will try to find alternative routes. If these routes cannot be found, then a blockage will occur, and energy that cannot move and vibrate becomes inactive and negative – creating minor problems at first and major problems later.

The chakras, those vortices of energy that draw in life-force, also become blocked; the negative energy at these points look like tangled balls of wool.

Minor blockages are the cause of ordinary fatigue, suffered by so many people nowadays – because the energy body is only working at a quarter or half of its capacity. There are several ways in which these minor blockages can be dislodged and removed. Exercises such as walking, running, swimming, dancing, horse-riding or cycling are excellent methods. To be truly effective it should be an everyday habit, though in fact, any exercise is better than none.

The exercises described in *Mind Magic* that pull at the aura until all the 'hot' spots have been removed, are also very effective. If you remember, 'hot' spots in the body are a sign of congestion.

I was taught so many incredible things by this teacher – for instance, how to recognize illness in the energy body other than by the negative spots. Just by being close to someone, I could 'feel' whether or not the body was lacking in energy, I could feel the positive and negative emotions. It 'feels' as though a boulder has been put between us when sitting with someone with a closed mind.

This also explains why 'survival evidence' cannot be given to some clients.

'Knowing' was also accelerated. I found that just by being with someone, I 'knew' practically everything about them. It was almost as if I became that person. I was taught how to merge my whole energy counterpart and mind energy with those of another person. It was as though I could jump in and out at will, and was yet another example of how 'survival evidence' is given. It was certainly fascinating, and I'm afraid I became hooked for a while. My own life is very full and I have never been particularly interested in other people's lives, but with my newfound gifts I merged into other energy bodies to experience their emotions. This practice was stopped by a warning from above; I had overstepped the mark. The gifts I had been given were for the good of mankind and not something one 'played' with.

I was also shown how to harness and reshape energy, and I could feel energy for the first time. It felt rather like silk at first, but later on had the texture of smooth plastic. It was fascinating to 'see' it being pulled about and reshaping itself.

I was into my first six months of surgery, and was about to perform an operation when I realized that the usual 'light' was missing. Instead, a 'knowing' had taken its place and I knew exactly where to operate. I knew what I had to do and without any further instruction, and from that day on I was completely alone. I was elated. I had obviously passed with flying colours.

Everyone benefited from the operations even though some people were not completely cured. Every day was different, something exciting was happening all the time. It was the most inspiring time of my life.

Because of my reputation, I attracted patients with terminal diseases and those who had completely baffled the medical profession. Whilst healing some of these very sick people, I was told to take my hands away. On doing so, I saw spirit hands carrying out the operation. Although some of the procedures were extremely complicated, I was given instructions throughout and was therefore able to follow them through when I was faced with similar problems in the future. One of these procedures was to insert an energy tube into the lung, through the rib cage, and draw off congestion and fluid – as in the case of Alex's operation in the first chapter.

The next two years were hectic, and then something changed. I was told by my spirit teacher that I could dispense with the images of the tools and other apparatus, and work along the same lines but with a beam of mind energy similar to a laser beam. I was not shown how to do it; somehow I just knew. This new technique was quick, and so I was able to see more people. Since then I have carried out thousands of spirit operations over more years than I care to remember. All of them have been a joy and a source of intrigue to all concerned.

The type of operation I carry out is very different to those of the psychic surgeons in the Philippines, except for one thing. Although the psychic surgeons actually cut the physical body and take out all manner of objects, they do seal the cut with their finger. Of course, there are frauds, as in any other occupation, but there have been some incredible psychic surgeons. I was privileged to watch one of them performing an operation in London, during a public demonstration.

A woman with a very large cyst on her cheek volunteered to undergo an operation. The surgeon ran his finger over the cyst, and a cut appeared. He then removed a mass of jelly-like substance from the cut, then healed it with his finger. The woman did not appear to suffer any pain, and was left with sagging skin where the cyst had been.

While this operation was taking place I was standing beside a group of doctors who were talking among themselves. One of them remarked that if she had performed the same operation without anaesthetic, the patient would have been in agony. Nevertheless, they still did not believe what they had seen; I am sure they dismissed it as group hypnosis.

* * *

I would like to end this chapter with two exercises. The first will help you, the reader, to merge with other energy bodies so that you can understand and help others. The second will aid your 'knowing' – a tremendous advantage if you wish to succeed in life and if you want to be able to help others understand themselves.

Feeling

1 Choose a partner and sit opposite each other. Look intently into your partner's eyes for five minutes. When you have done that, study them closely from head to toe, taking in every detail, every expression. You are going to *become* that person.

2 Close your eyes and breathe deeply three times. As you do so think of yourself as the other person. Remember what they looked like. Feel yourself moulding into them until you believe that you are a major part of them.

3 Now sit quietly and allow yourself to absorb the feelings and emotions of the other person.

4 Open your eyes, and hold hands with your partner. Exchange information and find out how correct you have been.

5 Close your eyes, and breathe deeply three times. Then sit for two minutes, allowing your mind to become a blank. Open your eyes and blink several times to bring yourself back. Look around you and you will find objects seem more clearly defined.

This exercise will lead to a greater understanding in your relationship.

Knowing

1   Choose a partner with whom you have empathy. Ask them to sit on a chair, then stand behind them and place your hands on their shoulders.

2   Close your eyes and clear your mind by allowing it to wander or daydream.

3   Allow yourself ten minutes in this dream state, then bring yourself back to normal. Your partner can time you.

4   Sit down on a chair facing your partner and tell them the impressions you have received relating to any part of their life. It could be their emotions, their mental and physical state, or it might be clairvoyance for the future. Impart your 'knowing' as simply as possible and please, whatever you do, do not give any information that might distress them. These exercises are to help and understand others, not to worry them.

5   Smile at each other, then breathe deeply until you feel completely relaxed. Smiling always brings an instant rapport.

These exercises, practised regularly, will open your mind and aid your psychic development in a gentle way.

The next chapter will take you right into the heart of the *Mind Waves* phenomenon. I hope you enjoy it.

3

Hypnotherapy

I have practised hypnotherapy for fifteen years. I have been guided by a spirit hypnotist, and have had remarkable results, the majority of which involved healing.

Why was it necessary to use hypnotheraphy when most contact healings were so successful?

When stress becomes part and parcel of our everyday existence, the mind energy is drawn into the head, causing a pressure on the brain and body. This in turn creates physical and mental problems which are sometimes very difficult to heal because the compression is dense, and with ordinary contact healing it takes much longer to ease the pressure.

One lady came to me for healing suffering with a crippling arthritic condition. The healing energy would usually ease or cure this condition, but in this case nothing happened.

When she came for her next appointment, my spirit doctor told me to give her hypnotherapy. I asked her permission, and she readily agreed. I asked her to close her eyes and listen to my voice. Then I began to speak.

'I want you to know that you are standing in a garden. It is a sunny day, and you can feel the warmth of the sun as it eases the pain in your body.

'Walk to the end of the garden where you will find a lift. Step into the lift and close the door behind you.

'In the lift you will find a bell. Ring the bell and the lift will descend. When it stops, open the door and walk out.

'You will find yourself on a balcony overlooking the sea. On the balcony is a comfortable chair where you can sit and watch the waves breaking over the rocks.

'As the tide goes out, know that it is also taking your pain with it.'

At this point I saw faint wisps of energy leaving her body around the head and shoulders. I continued to talk to her, and observed what was happening. The wisps became clouds, and as they dispersed they were followed by waves of energy, completely blanketing out part of the room.

I knew that this was negative congestive energy leaving her body. There was so much of it – no wonder she had such terrible physical problems, which, in turn had caused her much mental anguish. I assured her that she would feel less pain on a day-to-day basis. I brought her back, via the lift, into the garden. I then asked her to open her eyes.

She could not move at all for the first few minutes, and then gradually began to move her arms and legs. She stood up about ten minutes later. Her first reaction was that she felt as though a ton had been lifted from her shoulders. I asked her if she was still in pain. She said that it was difficult to tell as she felt numb all over.

As she left, I asked her to call me if she improved in the next few days.

After two days she called me. Apparently her physical and mental conditions had dramatically improved. 'I don't know what you did to me,' she said, 'but I can move my fingers for the first time in years, and my knees are much better.'

What had happened to her during the hypnotherapy session?

Whilst I was speaking to her she became completely relaxed, perhaps for the first time in many years. In this state of deep relaxation, the mind begins to expand. It links with the mind waves of the healer and takes on their relaxed state of mind and healing qualities. This in turn allows the congestion to be released at a subconscious level.

When she was in this relaxed state I asked her to go down in a lift. If she had not been suffering from such severe arthritis, I would have asked her to walk down many steps.

Giving the patient the feeling that they are going down steps, or in a lift, frees the mind energy from its prison, leaving the physical body behind. This in turn releases enormous amounts of congested energy. As a result the patient will feel light-headed. The more relaxed the patient has become, the heavier their physical body will feel. At the end of a session, the patient cannot move until instructed to do so. This command brings the mind energy back to a normal state.

Used in this way, hypnotherapy can relieve and cure hundreds of problems that are caused by congestive negative energy.

I remember one gentleman who asked for my advice. He had been looking after his invalid mother for many years and this had created many problems for him. As a result, he suffered terrible migraine attacks at least three times a week.

I suggested hypnotherapy. He was not happy with the idea and asked if he could have contact healing instead. I explained that, although contact healing would probably clear the problem, it would take longer than hypnotherapy. I could see clairvoyantly that he was very congested and I knew that by giving him hypnotherapy it would save his time and mine. However, he did not agree, and so contact healing was given on three visits.

On the third visit, he told me that his migraine had practically disappeared. He was very impressed.

After the fifth visit he told me that he was cured. I had to inform him that I could still 'see' congested energy and that it had not cleared completely, but he decided that he need not visit me again.

Within eight weeks he was back. He was having migraines at the rate of two per week. This time he agreed to hypnotherapy. I gave him one session and he was completely cured.

Of course, there are times when it is inadvisable to give hypnotherapy, and I am always informed by my spirit hypnotist when this is the case. Sometimes I have been surprised by the decision, only to find out later that the person had a mental problem, albeit a small one.

I rely totally on the mind wave telepathy that I have with the spirit world on these occasions, and it has always been correct. It is extremely dangerous to use this form of healing unless you are guided by a spirit doctor or you are a qualified hypnotist.

What I do teach is self-relaxation. One has the same feeling of heaviness and being out-of-this-world, but you control it, and you have a safety button.

Try the following exercise. You will have a mental button to press if you want to opt out at anytime.

The Swimming Pool

1 Lie down on a bed, or preferably on the floor. Think yourself into a sunlit garden. Now feel the warmth of the sun pervading every part of your body, from your toes to the top of your head. When you have mastered this

visualization, your whole body should be completely relaxed.

2 Walk down to the end of the garden. There you will see ten steps. Walk down the steps as you count.

3 Here you will find yourself at the top of a steep slide. Climb on, and allow yourself to slide down, holding on to the rail. You can control the speed yourself. Remember your mental button if you want to opt out.

4 When you reach the bottom you will find yourself slipping into a warm swimming pool. As it is filled with sea water, you will feel yourself floating on the surface. Do not try to swim.

5 It is at this point that you give yourself auto-suggestion. Tell yourself that you do not wish to smoke, overeat, worry etc. In this state you can convince your subconscious of anything!

6 When you feel that you have spent enough time in your pool, simply press your mind button. You will find yourself in a lift which will carry you back to the top and deposit you at the bottom of the ten steps.

7 Walk up the steps as you count. Walk back up the garden and lie down on the spot where you started your journey. Perhaps you would like to mark it with a rose-bush.

Remember, you can always opt out of the exercise any time you wish by pushing your mental button. It would be advisable to do this when you are only a little way into the exercise for the first time, so that you will feel safe when you carry it through to the end.

In fact, why not use your mental button all the time to release you from stress and anxiety.

4

Atmospheres

'There is no such thing as energy dimensions,' a gentleman said at a dinner party I was attending.

'How can you prove this?' I asked. He turned to me. 'How can *you* prove it, especially as no-one can see these things unless they are psychic?'

'I did ask the question first,' I said, 'so would you like to reply, and then I will give you my answer?'

He looked put out. 'Anyone with any common sense knows it's a load of claptrap. If we all listened to people like you we'd all be barmy.'

Obviously, I was not going to get any sense out of the man at all. I looked at him. 'What sort of atmosphere was there when you came in here tonight?' I asked, and he looked relieved that the conversation had returned to normal.

'Well, actually, I thought it was a bit strained at first, thought the whole evening was going to be a wash out. I had the feeling our hosts had been quarrelling, but perhaps I was wrong.'

I smiled. 'I had the same feeling; although they greeted us with smiles, there was a bit of a hostile atmosphere.'

The gentleman leaned toward me. 'It's funny, you know, I can usually tell what's been happening in a room before I enter it. Sometimes it just doesn't feel right and I'd rather be at home, so I leave.' He was really into the swing of the conversation by now. I was smiling. 'What do you think causes you to have these feelings?'

He stroked his chin. 'I don't know, but I have always been able to sense atmospheres.'

By this time I felt rather naughty, it was like leading a lamb to slaughter. But I felt mischievous, so I continued. 'What do you think creates those atmospheres, after all it isn't something you can see?'

He had caught on and glared at me. 'You're back to this energy rubbish again, aren't you?'

'Well, yes I am,' I replied, 'because in fact, it is mind energy that creates atmospheres. It can be a single or collective mind energies but the vibrations or waves of those energies are what you feel when you enter a room. In addition, a psychic can usually tell exactly what has caused the atmosphere. It's a knowing.' I continued with a smile. 'It seems to me that you have a gift for detecting mind waves. What a pity you won't recognize it.'

'I'm leaving, good evening,' he said, and got up from the table. 'Time I went home. Can't do with all this rubbish.'

I must confess I had been enjoying myself at his expense, and he knew it. It is quite absurd how some people dismiss things they cannot see whilst admitting they exist. It is only when they are brought face-to-face with the facts that they can see their arguments have no foundation.

Atmospheres are created by waves of mind energies. Everyone can sense there is an atmopshere, even if they are not able to ascertain the cause.

When someone is angry, their mind energy expands, as anger is a very positive state of mind. As it expands it causes waves of energy rather like shock waves and it is these vibrations that one can feel. The same thing applies to a person who is excited. There would be an aura of excitement around them. If a person is miserable, then their mind energy would be drawn in, absorbing energy from those around them rather like a vampire sucking blood. That is why one feels exhausted in the company of these people. Being with someone who is depressed can actually cause depression in others. I have spent many miserable evenings with people who are negative, and have been quite relieved when it was time to leave. Although some of them were perfectly nice people, they created an unpleasant atmosphere.

I have never met anyone who has ever been interested in analysing atmosphere, perhaps because we all live with it, and it is a major part of our lives. Yet it is very much a mind energy problem, and one that cannot be seen by people in general.

Awareness of these waves can be of tremendous help to one's career or emotional life. It can bring a greater understanding of what you are up against when things are going wrong, and how to react when they are right. So many people mess up their lives because they are unable to read the waves correctly.

How many times have you misread the vibrations that you were getting from your partner, and in so doing have created a bad atmosphere because of jealousy and suspicion – when, in fact, they were only figments of your own imagination?

How many times have you trusted your partner when you have had cause to be jealous or suspicious, and in so doing have been badly hurt?

No-one can be correct all the time, and many of us are hopeless when it comes to handling our own emotional affairs, but being aware of the atmosphere that mind waves can create can keep us one step ahead.

Collective mind waves are also immensely powerful and crowds of people can be completely carried away on waves, for both good and bad. Obviously, this can be dangerous, as we have seen with the problems that are created at football matches.

The majority of people who go to these matches are peaceful. They go to back their team, and release their adrenalin with high spirits. But if there is a group there that is bent on trouble, then their obsessive thoughts can be powerful enough to disrupt those around them; creating waves that sooner or later bounce off everyone at the match.

Many young people have been caught up in this atmosphere, and have created havoc and have done things which normally would have been totally alien to them. On reflection, they have been unable to understand their actions.

This is why it is so important to be aware of the vibrations that are created by others, and of the terrible damage they can cause.

On the bright side, when crowds gather at open air concerts an atmosphere develops which affects everyone present and raises the energies of even the most depressed personalities. For example, at the wonderful concert given by Pavarotti in Hyde Park in 1991 in the pouring rain, everyone was carried along on a wave of enjoyment and appeared oblivious of the atrocious weather and discomfort.

This kind of energy has great healing potential.

We usually believe that we know our families quite well, but there are hidden depths in everyone. If a member of the family is hiding something, or merely being negative, then they can change the atmosphere of a home in one day. This change will be obvious to everyone living in that home. That is why, in these circumstances, members of the family are constantly asking each other if there is anything wrong. It is not an expression or attitude that has prompted the question, but the vibrations.

I have known people who have been happy and healthy when living at home, and yet when they have left home to live with friends or a partner their personalities have changed. They have become miserable, morose, negative – and consequently suffer long bouts of ill health. The suggestion that their friend or partner has caused this change will usually be received with derision, and all sorts of excuses made. When the relationship ends, that person usually returns to normal.

No matter how much we may love someone, if it changes your personality completely and you are constantly unhappy or unhealthy, then it is time to think seriously about the rest of your life.

Many people have solved this problem by living apart but still keeping their relationship on a sound basis. Indeed many professionals have found that this is the only way to maintain a relationship. It gives both parties time to think and work.

When divorce has become inevitable parents may find it easier to preserve the friendship and family feeling when apart, and children can feel secure knowing that they are loved by both parents. Changing your life is no simple matter, but it can be worth the effort if you are happier and healthier.

Learn to read the vibrations you are receiving from the atmosphere, at a gathering, or from one or two persons – remembering, at the same time, that you can *change* the atmosphere.

Try the following simple exercise. This is for those of you who actually go out to work.

Absorbing the Atmosphere

1 When you walk into the office, factory, shop, etc., stand still for two minutes and absorb the atmosphere. Close your eyes if this is possible.

2 Try not to think. Keep your mind as blank as possible, and just feel. If the vibrations are unfriendly, then you will probably start feeling as though your stomach is knotting or at least bubbling. This is a very common feeling in this type of working environment.

3 If you feel as though something exciting is going to happen, then it is a very positive atmosphere.

4 Perhaps you will feel nothing at all. This may be because you have become accustomed to a fairly humdrum sort of atmosphere.

5 If there is a sense of foreboding, something may be about to happen, so keep an eye on everything going on around you on that particular day.

It is surprising how many people have been able to prevent a catastrophe just by being aware.

Energy Waves

This second exercise is for those of you who stay at home, whether you are a housewife or run your business from home.

1 About mid-morning, choose a peaceful room and sit quietly for about ten minutes.

2 During this time allow your mind to become a blank,

and absorb the atmosphere by simply allowing yourself to become part of it.

3 Feel yourself being drawn into the atmosphere and become aware of the waves of energy surrounding you.

4 These waves of energy will gradually be impressed upon your psyche, and you will become aware of the vibrations that exist in your home.

5 If you do not like the feeling you are receiving, then you must make an effort to bring more laughter and happiness into your life and home.

6 If you are content with the feeling and are happy with it, then you must ensure that your partner is happy with it when they come home.

How can you guarantee that your partner is happy with the feeling in your home? It is quite simple: ask them. I think you may be surprised at the answers, but it is a very good exercise for clearing away the cobwebs that may exist in a relationship.

If either of you feel too embarrassed to talk about problems that may exist, then write letters to each other. That can also be an eye-opener.

Everyone should practise the art of becoming a part of the environment in which they work, live or play. Sensitivity is increased and this endears you to friends and family. It is well worth the effort.

5

Automatic Writing

Automatic writing is when the author supposedly receives messages from spirits and writes them down, and is an area where there is much unconscious fraudulence. I have seen masses of correspondence believed to have been given by entities, but which was nothing of the sort.

The authors have been extremely genuine, and believed that it was true spirit communication, but I knew them all extremely well, and their personality and beliefs came through in the writing like a beacon, no matter how hard they had tried to cover up.

It is so very easy to fall into this trap.

Whilst I was sitting at a desk many years ago I heard a voice telling me to pick up a pen and write. This I did. I wrote a very long epistle simply by listening to the voice in my 'ear'. I thought at the time that the person communicating had the same ideas as myself and that I had found a spirit friend who would be able to help me in my work, but when I read the piece I realized that I had somehow linked into my higher mind. There was nothing I did not already know.

It is easy to see how people can deceive themselves, because one does actually hear a voice.

Perhaps I can explore this further. The higher mind is that part of the mind energy that is furthest from the physical body – part of the soul energy – and there are times, particularly when psychics are at the beginning of their career, when they can 'tune in' to a particular frequency in their own mind energy.

Just as the mind of someone deceased can communicate through a medium, so can one's own mind, given that part of it – the higher self and soul – is in another dimension.

Why is it that we do not recognize our own voices? The answer is simple – it is probably the first time we have heard our own spirit voice, and it was not expected.

It is rather like receiving an unexpected telephone call. It is more difficult to recognize the voice than it is when the call has been expected.

I am often telephoned at home, and usually I recognize the different voices, especially when they belong to my friends. But on occasion I have been waiting for a specific call and answering the telephone have 'recognized' the voice on the other end only to discover that it is someone entirely different.

It is very easy to fall into the trap of 'expectations'.

How does one know when automatic writing is genuine and is being given by spirit entities?

This is a difficult question to answer because every medium is different. It is a matter of honesty and principles.

First of all, one has to look at the quality of writing one is receiving. Is it going to help mankind in some way? Does it contain new philosophies that could help the world and give us more understanding of the Universe and Universal Law?

Does it provide a breakthrough that will prove to the sceptics, once and for all, that there is life after death?

I am sure that there is a mountain of genuine spirit communication through automatic writing, but I wonder why it has made so little impact upon us. Perhaps it is most difficult to believe because of the interaction of higher mind and spirit.

If you are receiving automatic writing, then you owe it to yourself to be absolutely honest. Is the type of information you are receiving worth the time that you spend actually writing it? Would it not be more worthwhile to spend your time and energies on healing the sick? Or giving genuine survival evidence?

If you answer these questions honestly, and still believe that the information you are receiving through writing is worthwhile, then discipline yourself so that you do not waste time. Do not write for more than one hour at a time – it can be very tiring.

Make an appointment with your communicator to work at the same hour every day. This will help both sides. After all, they will have other things to do in their dimension. If the appointment has to be cancelled for any reason, let your helper know beforehand. You may say that they will know in advance, and I agree. But good manners are always appreciated.

I do not believe that anyone, whether amateur or professional, should sit for hours waiting to see whether anyone wishes to communicate with them. My own experience has proved that when someone wishes to communicate they will do so – they simply don't leave you alone. And the communication is often so powerful it cannot be ignored.

When I wrote *Mind Energies and Positive Thought*, a little booklet that has helped hundreds of people all over the world, I knew nothing of how positive and negative thought could affect the mind energy. I had quite a few problems of my own at the time and happened to get up at 5 o'clock one morning to make myself a cup of tea. Whilst

I was drinking my tea, lost in thought, I heard a voice asking me to write. I put my cup down, listened, and wrote the booklet. When I had finished, I read what I had written. Those words changed my life.

It was full of plain common sense, something that I needed at that time. I read it every day for a month. I loved it. I happened to show it to a friend, and he liked it so much he suggested that I should have it made into a little booklet so that the words could help others. This took some time to arrange, but fourteen years and thousands of copies later, it is still being carried around in pockets and handbags throughout the world.

This was a genuine spirit contact.

I also received genuine spirit clairvoyance through automatic writing over a period of ten years. At the time, I laughed at the apparent absurdity of the information; it all seemed too far-fetched. Yet it all came true.

If you are receiving automatic writing, it is worth keeping and reading from time to time. Be honest with your analysis of it, ask yourself whether the information is really new or whether you had a notion about it before you wrote the piece.

If you have had clairvoyance, then of course, you must keep the notes to find out whether it has been correct. But whatever you do, don't *assume* it is correct.

With all mediumship, one has to be absolutely truthful to oneself. If mediums begin to fool themselves, then it is time for them to give up – sooner or later their reputation is bound to suffer.

One must not dismiss communication from one's higher mind as inferior – it can sometimes be most enlightening. The wording is simple and straight to the point, and highlights the different shades of our personality. Being brought face to face with our true selves can be most enlightening and sometimes frightening, but it does enable us to improve our image.

I find automatic writing from composers really fascinating. Rosemary Brown, a very well-known and respected medium, has received compositions from famous composers that have been authenticated by top musicologists, and some of these works have been played by equally famous orchestras. She is a very talented medium indeed.

I have known many psychic children receive automatic writing, although they themselves are unaware of this. I am sure that if nurtured and allowed to have a normal childhood, they will grow up to be fine mediums and healers. One little boy I know will, I am sure, be a fine musical medium when he is older.

Parents are far more intelligent when dealing with their psychic children than they used to be. They do not want to bring attention to them, and that is the correct way to handle the situation. What these children need in abundance is understanding and love.

If *you* are receiving automatic writing, then please do not allow your imagination to run away with you and be as honest as possible. To thine own self be true.

A word of warning. If you receive any messages that are frightening, stop immediately, put pen and paper away, and forget them. It may be that you are in a distressed or low condition and are thus attracting the wrong kind of spirits.

Above all, keep your sense of humour. Automatic writing can help to sort problems out and keep you earthed. Have fun!

6

Wild Animals and Pets

I have communicated with animals all my life. As a child, I used to feel the pain and distress of the strays as they roamed the streets of London, unloved and under-nourished.

One day, whilst stroking a particularly mangy cat that was sitting on a wall, I sensed that it was unhappy. I started to speak to it as a friend, and told it that it would soon feel well and loved. After a few minutes there seemed to be a feeling of peace around us. At that time I had no idea what was happening, and as a child, one does not analyse these things. Obviously, it had been healing energy that had enveloped us. I also felt that I knew the cat's thoughts. I remember being aware of its need for love and understanding.

The memory of this experience has remained with me all my life. I now understand mind energy, and I realize that the feelings I had were the first stages of telepathy, where mind energy waves ripple and mix with other minds.

Children are incredible. When they talk to their pets they know they are being understood, and they also hold apparently imaginary conversations with them. They are, of course, having a telepathic conversation, even if they themselves are unaware that something quite extraordinary is happening. They accept these things. It is only as adults that they begin to feel self-conscious and secretive, and lose that wonderful innocence and acceptance of natural law.

The majority of human beings belittle the capacity of animal mind energy. Animals are treated as inferior to man, and yet when given loving care and coaching they can perform extraordinary telepathic feats.

Cats in particular have a natural capacity for finding their way around. If they do not like a particular home environment they will seek another home with caring people. Their actions are always instinctive.

And how many times have you heard of a cat finding its way back to its old home when it has been taken hundreds of miles away to a new home? More important, how do you think it achieves this?

The answer to these questions is mind waves. The cat has only to project its mind energy to the vicinity of its old home for there to be an immediate energy link; all the cat has to do is follow the beam.

They are also one of the most relaxed of animals. Some of the yoga exercises were based on the cat species. Why *are* they so relaxed? I believe it is their independent spirit, the freedom they desire and demand.

Cats who are locked in flats and houses all day and night are usually sick, mentally and physically. They need space and the ability to get out whenever they wish, so that they can patrol their own territory.

Humans are more adaptable – we allow our spirit or mind to be locked up, although restlessness is there all the time under these conditions, and as a species we cannot relax. I believe we should take a leaf out of the cat's book and try, as individuals, to be more independent, to demand space.

The media brings us face-to-face with the facts of

cruelty to animals, and because of this there has been an extraordinary change of attitude. Wonderful work is now being done all over the world to combat this.

Not enough, though, has been written about animals' sensitivity, about their intuition and the love and care they show each other and humans.

A typical example of their love towards humans are the stories of wolves caring for abandoned human babies. Their reputation as killers has not been upheld in recent surveys.

The senseless cruelty that is dealt out to animals in general is far more tragic than the world realizes. Millions of people all over the world turn a blind eye to cruelty to animals in the wild. It is not on their doorsteps, so why should they worry?

But there is an enormous amount of animal suffering on our own doorsteps that even these people should not disregard and much of this is the result of pure ignorance.

Animals have an instinctive knowledge of how to heal themselves. They will find a quiet, safe place and sleep until they recover or seek a sympathetic human to help them.

Pets are also extremely sensitive to adult emotions, and they sense when there are problems within the household. Arguments upset them, and in such circumstances dogs, especially, will crawl on their belly trying to find somewhere to hide. When the argument is over they will often come out and tap each person with their paw to show how pleased they are.

One only has to look into the eyes of an animal to know what kind of life it has, to see the happiness or the broken spirit.

I would like to bring everyone's attention to the power of individual and mass mind energies of all creatures, and also to their incredible memory; they never forget a kindness and they never forget when they have been hurt. Perhaps this knowledge will help to alleviate the misery some of them suffer through man's ignorance.

When I was in my teens, my brother brought home a small black mongrel dog – a genuine Heinz variety – and gave it to me as a present. I was overjoyed at having my own dog. She was beautiful and loving. One day she got out of the front gate, and as I ran after her an old man with a stick first kicked her and then hit her with his stick. She yowled with pain. After checking that she was not seriously hurt, I made a fuss of her and several days later forgot about the incident. Unfortunately, she did not. Whenever an old man with a stick came along she tried to bite him. This hatred remained with her for the rest of her life, and yet in every other way she was still loving and gentle.

I had an acquaintance whose husband always stroked their dog and made a fuss of it whilst my friend was present. She could never understand why the dog did not like him and why it crawled away on its belly every time he was near it. Her husband complained bitterly that he had tried hard to make friends with it. Neighbours, however, knew differently. Every time my friend went out, he kicked the dog and left it howling outside in all weathers. Eventually his cruelty was exposed and my friend gave up work to be with her pet all the time. She eventually left her husband.

I could never attend a circus when I was a child, because I used to feel the despair of the animals. When I complained, I was told that they were happy. No doubt it was easier to assume that they were happy because it suited the owner's purpose to use them in this way to make money.

Money is the greatest evil of all. It is very rarely used to the advantage of those who are in need – especially where animals are concerned.

In the guise of sport, men on horseback with more money than sensitivity chase foxes across the countryside in order to see them being ripped apart by hounds. Deer trapped by a circle of hounds send out terror-stricken mind waves that would break the heart of sensitive people. Yet their hunters do not care.

One can only hope that their children will care, and that more humane methods will be used to kill animals if their numbers need to be checked.

I believe that this question should be put to the nation. Ordinary people, with common sense and sensitivity, should have their say. After all, landowners do not own the spirit of the wild creatures that live upon their land. We should be nurturing them and protecting them – instead we have taken away their food and their space.

So many humble creatures have disappeared through man's inhumanity. A noble creature whose numbers are declining is the elephant. That is why I have selected an excerpt from Mark Shand's book *Travels on my Elephant* (Jonathan Cape, 1991), a story which tells of his journey across India on an elephant named Tara.

Through the driving rain we could just make out the blurred outline of the Dhauli hills. On top of a prominent hillock, blinding white against a black sky stood the Vishwa Shanti Stupa, the domed Peace Pagoda the Buddhists built in this century with Japanese collaboration, to commemorate the conversion to Buddhism of the great Indian Emperor Ashoka.

We took a short cut across some open fields to the River Daya, a river which was said 'to have run red with blood' during the horrifying slaughter of the battle of Kalinga, a massacre so enormous that Ashoka flung away his blood-stained sword and embraced the path of peace. It was on these very fields that the great battle had been fought. Under the black rainclouds, it was a black and eerie place. The wind moaned soulfully, pushing into us and making us shiver, less from the cold than from something else, perhaps the spirits of the one hundred thousand souls that had been slaughtered here. Tara sensed it too. She moved forward reluctantly, her trunk in the air, sensing, probing. Finally she came to a halt. Bhim tried to urge her and she let out a loud reverberating roar which I could only imagine was of terror. With her ears extended fully forward, she backed hurriedly away, then turned and fled.

'Mummy no like it here,' Bhim yelled over his shoulder, struggling to gain control.

'Let's get out of here,' I muttered to Aditya.

'God knows how many elephants perished in this spot,' Aditya replied, shivering. 'This is an elephants' graveyard. After two and a half thousand years how is it possible Tara still senses that?'

Somehow I believe it possible.

It is a story which illustrates my beliefs. Elephants are particularly sensitive creatures, and the mind waves of elephants massacred on this scale would indeed instil terror into Tara.

These terror-stricken mind waves experienced by the slaughtered elephants are encapsulated in the earth and the ether for ever.

Can you imagine what must be in the ether in Africa, where elephants have been slaughtered and whole herds nearly wiped out just for ivory? Those wonderful, noble creatures killed solely for man's greed.

And can you also imagine the terrible vibrations this ivory must have absorbed at the time of the killing? It can only bring bad luck to the people who buy it, as the vibrations will be there for ever – as they are in the concentration camps such as Auschwitz. Those places are bereft of life. No creatures would enter those areas, even long after they had been deserted. What other reason could there be for this phenomenon than that the vibrations are too bad for animals to inhabit the area?

I have always been devastated at the terrible cruelty inflicted on chickens in batteries, and never more so than when I visited an agricultural college near my home on an open day.

It was a pleasant sunny day and I was enjoying myself, but then I suddenly began to feel ill. I recognized the feeling immediately – there were distressed animals somewhere around.

I saw people walking out of a shed, looking ill. I was about to peer in when my daughter said, 'Don't go in there. It will upset you.' I *did* look in and I will never forget what I saw: chickens with no feathers on their necks, rubbed off as they tried to reach for food, and jammed in by other chickens. There was no room to move or sit down. It was sickening, and I won't try to describe any more.

I turned to the people I was with and said, 'Their tortured minds will come back and kill us.' I repeated this to as many people as I could, and I knew it would happen. Whatever we give out we will receive back tenfold or more.

One man said, 'How can a load of chickens kill humans?' I told him he had a lot to learn. Two years after this episode there were cases of illness and death from salmonella and other terrible bacteria present in chickens and their eggs.

Scientists would say that it was because of the filthy food the chickens were fed – their dead mates, for example. I know that is only part of the real truth.

A terrible revenge can be wrought by the collective mind waves of animals. Do not dismiss this power. It is very real.

68

I am pleased to report that the agricultural college in question now has free-range chickens. At least they have learned from the experience.

Another time, whilst holidaying in Madeira, I decided to join a coach trip around the island. I do not really like coach trips, because I prefer to look at scenery in a relaxed and peaceful way, but with no car at my disposal it was my only choice. It was a beautiful day, and I was feeling relaxed and happy.

Out of the blue I had the same sick feeling as before, although I couldn't see anything to make me feel this way, just hills and little sheds. So why this awful feeling?

The courier was talking about the people and animals of the country, and she explained that all the little sheds that we could see each housed a cow. I immediately thought that this could not be possible as they were too small. She continued, 'This is the best meat you will taste on this island. It is very tender. This is because the cow never sees daylight and cannot stand because it has no muscles. It is kept purely for the manure, and eventually, the meat.'

The cows were fed several times a day, and the manure used for the land. Then they are killed for their meat. The courier was euphoric about the delights of eating such tender meat.

What she did not know was the misery that was being digested with the meat. Every single morsel would be impregnated. It is no wonder that the human race is so sick.

After this experience, my holiday was a disaster. My mind constantly went back to these poor creatures, and I vowed never to visit that country again. At least not until these sort of practices are dead.

On a happier note, I would like to give two different examples of how the mind waves of animals work. The first extract is from Valerie Porter's book *Faithful Companions: The Alliance of Man and Dog* (Methuen, 1987). The extract describes something that happened during the Second World War.

A mongrel by the name of Flak was the grounded mascot of a bomber crew in Tunis. He always came on to the airfield just before 'his' crew's plane returned – he had unerring timing. One day he came on to the field and set up a mighty howling; he knew, before anyone else did, that the crew had just been shot down over Italy.

There are numerous stories of dogs who were aware of the death of their soldiers, sailors and airmen hundreds or thousands of miles from home.

I read once of a dog who found its way across the channel to the trenches in France during the First World War. It also found its owner there. How?

If you have never believed in mind waves I think you will have to think again after you have read this book.

I have experienced several times the phenomenon of dogs howling when relatives of their owners have died suddenly, even when they are some distance away.

The second extract is from Matthieu Ricard's *The Mystery of Animal Migration* (Constable, 1969).

Some cats were taken from a town and placed in darkened containers and then transported some miles away after a most complicated journey full of detours and retracing steps. There was no possibility that the cats could use their memory of the route for this experiment. The cats were then taken from the containers and placed in the centre of a large maze with twenty-eight exits.

The great majority of cats chose the exit that was in the direction of their home.

Creatures can also be aware of imminent earthquakes. People have seen an exodus of wild and tame animals several days before the earthquake happens. The most sensitive of these animals will pass on their frightened mind waves to the others, and they panic collectively. Humans in these areas are well aware of this phenomenon, and use it as a guide as to whether or not they should leave their homes – even though there are as yet no outward signs of a disaster and no warnings have been given out over television or radio.

Normally peaceful dogs have been known to howl when their sick owner has died in hospital.

There can be no question that there is an interaction of something unseen between human beings and animals. Telepathy is the only way one can harness this energy. It is also the only answer to understanding what animals need and require to make life on this planet a happier place.

They do not understand our language, and yet we talk to them for hours. How much easier it would be to send them telepathic messages that they could understand. Telepathy is a universal language.

It may sound far-fetched, but telepathic communion with animals has been practised for centuries, especially in close relationships that men have had with their working dogs.

Sheepdogs in particular have an uncanny 'knowing'. That is because the owners spend an enormous amount of time with them when young. Although they obey spoken commands and respond to whistles, it goes far beyond that.

It is the time spent with the young animals that has the most effect; in that time, a process of exchanged mind waves has been established.

My own bitch, Tessa, has a favourite chair by the fire. It is also by the telephone. I have only to think about making a call, and she will leave the chair as I enter the room. However, if I come in for any other reason she will stay put.

She is sensitive to every thought. I can spend hours in the kitchen, and she won't take any notice until I reach for a can of dog food. Before it is out of the cupboard she will be standing in the kitchen waiting to be fed.

One night, my husband Alan had gone to bed, and Tessa began to bark. He waited to see if she would stop but she didn't. He went downstairs and calmed her, then crawled back to bed. Before he could go to sleep she started barking again. Once more, he reassured her that everything was all right. By this time his thoughts were only of sleep.

He eventually fell asleep only to have an awful nightmare. He was in a strange room with many doors; as he shut one door another would open. He woke up in a sweat only to hear Tessa barking again.

He went downstairs again, thoroughly fed up by this time. Thinking that perhaps Tessa wanted to go out he opened the back door. As he did so he heard the creaking of the side door that led to the garage. The wind was so strong, the door would have been torn off its hinges had it been left unlocked all night. Yet it could not be heard from inside the house.

Tessa was determined that she was going to make contact with her master, and she did this by giving him mind pictures of doors that needed to be shut.

I could recount hundreds of stories where I have cured animals with absent healing. Again, this is a typical example of telepathic contact. I have even been able to tell the owners what their animals are thinking. This has led to many a hilarious conversation, but has resulted in a better life for the animals.

Why not try to give your own animals a bit more consideration by having telepathic contact with them. At the end of this chapter you will find exercises to help you to do this.

Animals, like people, also communicate collectively.

Time and again, they have suffered hate and fear campaigns. Many of these are justified, especially where unsuitable dog owners have allowed their animals to savage people and to run amok. But there are owners all over the world who are responsible and caring, who own similar dogs who are perfect pets and delightful animals. Yet these unsuspecting owners and their pets have to submit to all kinds of humiliating nonsense because of the ignorant few.

Why do seemingly well-behaved pets suddenly go berserk? That is a very difficult question to answer. The fact is that they do, and we all have to try to handle the consequences.

Pedigree dogs seem to be the most aggressive in these outrages. I believe that the problem in these cases is extreme sensitivity, caused by inbreeding. This leads to an imbalance of mind and body, not found in ordinary mongrels.

There is a collective unconscious that affects every breed of dog. When one of a certain breed commits a terrible act of aggression it is plastered all over the newspapers and will appear on radio and television. Rightly so! But this can lead to a hate campaign, and the collective minds of people seeing this will reach out and affect the whole of that breed nationwide. People also feel fear when meeting one of the breed in the street, even if the dog is old and docile. The dog will pick up these vibrations and will be unnerved by them; if it is a young dog it could be so disturbed that it would display an aggressive reaction. From this point it is all downhill. More of the breed begin to act aggressively, because they are collectively absorbing aggressive vibrations and therefore become very disturbed. Seemingly loving dogs can become very aggressive, much to the horror of their owners.

This is not mere theory. I have studied this phenomenon over many years: as soon as different breeds receive waves of fear and hate they react accordingly.

I believe that people can act too hastily – especially when an animal is supposed to be a health hazard. For example, in recent years, badgers were hunted and gassed by so-called experts because they were apparently a hazard to people and cattle. There will always be scares of this nature, some of which are true and some are not. It is hasty decisions that anger me. After all we do not get rid of people who are contagious. Perhaps we need more thought and less hysteria.

Badgers are still hunted and killed in the dead of night by thugs who cannot live without the sight of violence and blood, and who use the reasons above as an excuse. Where is the media now? Perhaps we should have a badger love campaign, and similar campaigns to help all animals whose space we have so conveniently occupied. Always remember, they were here first.

There was an article in a newspaper recently about cats having a type of leukaemia. It was also reported, correctly, that this could not be passed on to humans, and yet I had many telephone calls from people asking if they would be safer if they had their cats put to sleep. I just could not believe it.

It is so easy to stir up adverse reactions to animals. We

74

must all be more responsible in our thoughts, and remember that they are being received by people and animals alike. Mass mind energies can create hysteria in both species.

Now to something more pleasant. If you would really like to have telepathic communication with your special animal, read on.

If you have more than one pet, try the following exercise on them one at a time.

Communicating With Your Pet

1 Wait for a time when your pet is asleep. It is much easier to reach the subconscious whilst it is in this state.

2 Close your eyes. Now speak to your pet telepathically. Use the same technique as though you were speaking normally – the only difference is that you will hear the words in your head. Have a loving conversation and assure your pet of your love and respect. Tell it that you will do everything in your power to give it a happy and contented life. Just keep talking. No effort is required; thoughts travel much faster without an impetus behind them.

3 Ask for its cooperation in assisting you by ridding itself of bad habits. Give your reasons as you would if you were speaking to a human.

4 When you have tried this exercise every day for a week, go on to the next exercise.

Telepathic Communication

With this exercise, you can use telepathic communication

with as many animals as you wish. They will all pick up the vibrations.

1 This is specifically for pets who go out for walks, and in this exercise you will be speaking to your pets whilst they are awake. The first step is taken when you are about to take them for a walk. Look them straight in the eyes and say telepathically, 'Would you like to go for a walk?' Watch the reaction. If they start to wag their tails or rush to the door, then you know that you have reached them. If there is no reaction, try again, but not for more than five minutes. If you get no response at all, then take the animal or animals out for a walk and try another time. Remember, both you and your pets are new to this exciting game, so take it in easy stages.

2 When you return from the walk, look at your pet or pets, and ask them to go and lie down. You may find they will do this anyway, but if you have a particularly active dog, like my own, they will jump up and down to the last, hoping to entice you outdoors again. With this type of animal, telepathy can be very successful. As you know your pets so well, you will also know when you are successful.

Communication Through Visualization

1 This is for cats and any other kind of pet. When they are active, talk to them telepathically. If you would like them to stop wrecking your home, then ask them in the nicest possible way. Because cats are so independent, you will have to be very patient and it may take time, but with perseverance you can have good results. You can simply pass on your loving thoughts to the animal and they will feel the vibrations and be more content.

2 When your cat has been out for some time, use telepathy to ask it to return. Let it know that you are going to feed it. Food is always a sure way of enticing animals back home.

3 Visualize the food that you are going to give, then visualize the cat eating it. If your pet does not return the first time, keep trying. The rewards are well worth the effort involved.

Why not use your imagination and visualize your own scenes and reactions. Once you have found the right formula for this talent, try others. You will find it extremely worthwhile.

PART TWO

PROJECTION OF
MIND WAVES

7

The Regression Phenomenon

What is the regression phenomenon? It is receiving information about past lives. This comes to me in two ways. First, through survival evidence, and second, in a more spectacular way when an energy face manifests over a normal physical face. These energy faces are very rarely anything like the normal face of that person.

I mentioned transfiguration in my previous book *Mind Magic*. That is when faces manifest over the face of the medium, and members of the audience recognize, and indeed have conversations with, friends and family who have died. The faces I see building up are manifesting themselves over the faces of ordinary people, people who are not even psychic.

When this phenomenon began I had no warning, and indeed had no idea how to discipline it. At first, both the client and I were so excited that it was a case of downing tools no matter what we were doing, so that we could look and listen to what was happening. Unfortunately, this interfered so much with my life that I sent messages out into the Universe, asking for it to be disciplined. Months later, the manifestations occurred only at convenient times for both myself and my clients or friends. It has become disciplined over the years and is consequently of a superior quality.

I cannot *make* manifestations happen. But I do have a

warning when it is about to take place. Excitement wells up within me, rather like the feeling when one is about to receive a present. Within five minutes the faces begin to build up, and when they are fully materialized I start to receive information, either by actually hearing a voice or by telepathic communication.

Perhaps the next story will enlighten you a little. A friend of mine came to spend the evening with me, and we were sitting by the fire, warm and relaxed, when I just happened to mention how lovely it was to have an evening off. She agreed. As she spoke, I looked at her and was about to continue the conversation when I saw a transparent mist covering her face. I told her what I could see, and she said, 'I can feel something like a spider's web on my face. This is really eerie – what is happening?' As I was familiar with the phenomenon I was able to put her mind at rest, and described the face that was now covering her own. I asked her to sit quietly, and I was then given information of a previous life in the year 1878. That person was telling me, through telepathic communication, about her life in that year. She was twenty years old, and worked as a maid in the country. I was shown a cobbled yard and what looked like a cow shed. She told me that this was her home and that it was bitterly cold as they had no heat at all – only that from the big oil lamps. Her name was Mary. Through all of this, the energy face was animated, changing all the time. Suddenly, my friend's voice said, 'I am so cold.' Although her voice sounded normal, it had a dreamlike quality. I began to ask her questions, and then she said, 'It's funny – I feel as though I am still here, but I can feel and see things as though I am dreaming.' I asked her to tell me about the pictures she was getting, and she described the cobbled yard and the house, and told me that she had to hold her hands above old oil lamps to keep warm. At this point she was not aware of the telepathic conversation I had had with Mary. My friend became quiet, and Mary's communication began again, but this time I actually heard the voice of a young girl with a pronounced accent. I believe she came from Devon. 'I wanted to help', she said, 'because she is afraid of dying,' (meaning my friend). 'I was afraid of dying and yet when it happened it was so beautiful. I was in a big hall, and a lady who was dressed in white came and took me to her home and looked after me. She told me that I could take my time in deciding what I wanted to do with my life! So you see, I thought I should tell your friend not to be frightened, because we both exist within her mind.'

Mary's face started to disappear, and the communication ceased. My friend seemed to be half-asleep. I shook her gently, and she sat up. 'Oh! I'm so sorry,' she said. 'I must have dozed off.' I explained in detail what had happened. 'That's funny,' she told me. 'Although I felt I was asleep, I could hear my own voice. It was a very odd experience,' she went on. 'You know I always feel cold even in summer.' I asked her if she was afraid of death and she told me she was terrified. We sat and talked about the experience for about an hour, and then she left.

A week later she telephoned me to say, 'Betty, I have to tell you that I've lost all fear of death, and what's more I no longer feel the cold all the time.' She was delighted.

I had seen this sort of transfiguration for about a year at this time, and was quite blasé about it. So many things were happening that I had very little time to think about what had happened that evening or, indeed, of other similar experiences. There is one memory, though, that stayed with me for a very long time.

I was healing a man of about twenty-eight years of age. He had fair hair and rather a boyish round face, very pleasant in looks and personality. He had fallen asleep during the healing and a boy's face manifested over his. It was quite clearly Jewish, and during the next half-hour I was given a harrowing account of a child who had died in the gas chamber at Auschwitz. He described the terrible overcrowded conditions in the train on the journey to Auschwitz; no air, no lavatories, no water or food. He spoke about the terrible stench and the dead bodies. On arrival they were all separated from their parents and herded like cattle. He never saw his family again. He was naked when he went into the gas chamber, and he remembered the hunger and cold, and the relief when he found himself in a place of beauty, surrounded by love, after he had died. He said, 'Tell him,' indicating the man who was asleep, 'that his nightmares will be no more. That is all you must say.'

After the face and the messages had disappeared I sat quietly for a while. The account was so graphic that I felt that I had experienced it myself.

The young man awoke. 'I'm sorry,' he said, smiling. 'I must have dropped off. It was so peaceful – I wish I could sleep like that every night.' I asked him if he had nightmares. He said, 'Ever since I can remember I have had terrible nightmares about twice a week.' I asked if he could remember what they were about. He grimaced. 'Yes! It seems as though I am locked in, and can't breathe, as though I have asthma – which I don't. It really is very frightening, and when I wake up I always have to get up and make myself a cup of tea. Then the next morning I feel absolutely washed out.' I looked at him. 'I have a message for you,' I told him. 'You won't have that nightmare any more.' He smiled. 'What makes you think that? I can't see them disappearing after so many years.'

'I've been told to give you that message,' I said. 'We will

have to wait and see.' He left, but I was still pretty shaken by the whole thing and thought about it for a long time.

The voice I had heard was that of a child who had grown up very quickly, and who had seen and experienced unbelievable tragedy. The mind of that child was now part of the young man who had come for healing, and as our minds are everlasting, so are the memories of all of our lifetimes. The soul part of the mind needed to help that young man find peace by giving him a simple message. What it did *not* want to do was to revive those memories into the present memory.

Two weeks passed, and then I received a telephone message to say that the young man had had no more nightmares since his last healing session. He made an appointment to see me the following week.

He arrived early, and he was ecstatic. 'Do you know, I haven't had a single nightmare since I saw you last. Do you think I have been cured?' I smiled, and said that I thought only time would tell, but that it certainly looked promising. He laughed. 'I'll tell you something else. My sense of smell has improved. I've never been able to enjoy flowers because they all smelled the same, but now I can. It really is a miracle. I'm sorry to say this, but I don't think I will need you any more.' 'But what about your painful knees?' I asked. 'They're not painful any more. I'm telling you, the whole thing is a miracle.'

I gave him healing for the last time, and I never saw or heard of him again. He had obviously been completely cured.

I had similar evidence from another client when her grandmother came through giving a harrowing account of her time in a concentration camp. She told of beatings, freezing temperatures with little clothing – and what she did have were only rags. She described the terrible years and the tragedies in her life – which ended in the gas chambers.

When she came to the end of her story, she said, 'Since I came here,' – meaning the dimension she was in – 'I have learned of all my previous lives, and it has been a revelation. Things that do not seem to make sense when they happen in your dimension are all part of a whole, like pieces of a jigsaw. I have not been shown the whole, only certain parts, but even that makes more sense than it did. You see, when there are only a few thousand people suffering, then the world takes no notice at all. Only suffering on a gigantic scale will ensure that the whole world takes notice. That is why it is always too late. Until mankind understands unconditional love and responds to the few when they are in trouble, then these terrible tragedies will go on and on until the lesson is learned.

'I have had three violent deaths and I have been told that there will be no more, for which I am grateful. But I hope that in my new lives I will never forget, and that I carry love with me all the time.'

My client was in tears at this point, and her grandmother said, 'Forgive everything and everybody so that you can spread hope. Remember, in the end we all have to judge ourselves, and realize that we cannot escape from ourselves and what we have done. The mind is for ever.'

As in the previous case histories, my client sent me a letter afterwards telling me that the nightmares she had suffered, since her grandmother's death, had gone. She felt that all her tomorrows would bring a greater happiness.[1]

From that day I have never been contacted by any other

[1]Although there was no manifestation in this case, I thought the story should be told.

victims of Nazi persecution, and I feel very privileged to have been able to bring this information through to this dimension – especially as it brought such relief to the people who had sought help.

Those of you who have read *Mind to Mind* and *Mind Magic* will understand how I receive survival evidence. But exactly what is happening in the case of regression, when an energy face is formed over a normal face and both the client and myself receive information of a previous existence? It puzzled me for a long time, until I realized that excess psychic power coming from me was stimulating the mind energy of these people, to such an extent that part of their mind memory – belonging to a previous life – was being released to help them understand problems in their present life. In fact, it was all part of the healing process. In every case, and there have been hundreds, the person was cured of a long-standing problem with their health.

My research into mind energy and mind waves has spanned eighteen years. There will never be an end result, because there is no end to the incredible events created by this energy world.

The tragedy is that people in the so-called scientific world have no idea how to link into the source of these miraculous events, and, like everything else they do not understand, they dismiss them, losing out on the very basics of psychic science.

I believe the reason they are so dismissive of the subject is because we do not know how to make things happen at will. Things either happen or they don't. For instance, I can work for about eighteen months without anything new or exciting happening, and then I have a feeling of expectancy as though something is about to happen. And it does. I rarely know what it is going to be, but I do know that I have never been disappointed.

The story I am about to relate is another typical example of regression through survival evidence.

A client of mine was happily listening to her dead mother's evidence of survival, when suddenly her mother stopped communicating and I was shown mind pictures of a young girl of about eighteen desperately trying to beat out the flames on her nightdress. The bedroom was engulfed with smoke and flames. There were no windows, only a fanlight which she was unable to reach. She fell to the floor, and the last picture I saw was of her body being engulfed by the flames. I knew that the young girl was my client in a previous life, and I also knew that she was terrified of fire in this life. She confirmed this, and said, 'My family think I'm crazy. I cannot leave the house until I have made sure that all the gas taps are off. I refuse to have matches in the house in case someone leaves a lighted match around. I even keep the gas lighter for the fire in a steel box. I am terrified of fire. Now that I understand, perhaps I can come to terms with my problem. Unfortunately, I know my husband will never believe what you have said.'

'I don't think it matters whether he believes you or not, if it helps you to find peace,' I replied, and she agreed.

I did not hear from her for about a month, but when she did telephone, her voice was completely different, 'Betty,' she said, 'I am not completely cured, but I am well on the way. Thank you so much. I will never forget you.' She sent me a letter two months later to say that she was completely cured.

What an incredible world this Magical Universe is, these unseen dimensions that occasionally open their doors so that we can glimpse a fragment of what is beyond. Understanding is beyond our capacity at our present stage of evolution as human beings. All we can do is guess at what is really happening.

Regression Through Hypnosis

I have regressed several people through hypnosis but I did not enjoy the experience, so I did not pursue it.

A very famous hypnotist Joe Keeton, however, has successfully regressed thousands of people. In his book co-authored with Peter Moss, *Encounters with the Past* (Sidgwick & Jackson, 1979), I particularly like the chapter on reincarnation. Here is an extract:

Reincarnation is in many ways an attractive theory both in a general sense and as an explanation for hypnotic regression. It does, for example, present a fairly easily understood kind of immortality here on earth rather than in an abstract Heaven and Hell, and its kharma, the reward and punishment principle, seems to offer a logical answer to the injustices of what seems to be underserved human misery or privilege.

It can too perhaps explain the infant prodigy – a Mozart composing at five – and also the very common experience of *déjà-vu*. Almost everyone has come across the scene, a face or a piece of writing which is utterly familiar and yet which he can prove conclusively that he has never seen before. What is more natural than to accept that this belongs to a previous existence and that whatever has been handed on from one body to the next carried with it some memories of the past life.

If we can accept the principle of reincarnation at all, it does offer the simplest and most obvious explanation for the way in which a subject takes on a new personality in regression.

The reason I like this extract so much is that these are my beliefs exactly. However, there is one question. Do we also have genetic memory? If so, is there any point in reliving what might be the past life of an ancestor – especially if the experience is distressing? Having said that, I still believe that one should have freedom of choice.

I believe that Joe Keeton is the best man in his field. He

has passed numerous scientific tests and, if you are contemplating regression you would be well advised to put yourself into the hands of a man of this calibre.

In the next chapter I would like to take you into a world of reality, but it is a world which you might think is fantasy.

8

Ghosts and Spirits

Why are people so afraid of ghosts? I think the word itself is frightening, because we have been conditioned from birth to believe that ghosts are alarming. Just think of all the books and films about ghosts and how intentionally scary they are. In reality it can be very different, although people who have seen ghosts often say they were frightened out of their wits – probably because the encounter was unexpected and the atmosphere gloomy. It is far easier to see ghosts in the dark because energy is more distinguishable against a dark background.

Many people do not believe that ghosts exist, but I can assure you that they do. I have seen hundreds, and so have many other psychics. They are in fact nothing more than spirit people. They usually appear in older houses, and because they are not recognized by the current owners, they call them ghosts. If they were more recently deceased, and were recognized as being members of the family, they would call them spirits.

Of course, seeing a spirit is not as exciting as being able to tell people you have seen a ghost. Everyone loves ghostly stories. We all love being frightened to death, especially in the company of friends, sipping drinks around a log fire.

There are so many stories about sightings that I think we can safely say that ghosts do exist. Never mind the sceptics. I believe that the so-called psychic researchers would dismiss ghosts even if they themselves had seen one. After all, they have to keep up appearances.

I admire those who are courageous enough to admit to having seen a ghost or spirit. Being honest is far more admirable than moving along with the crowd. And it's not so boring!

So, ghosts are nothing more than old spirits, but why do they haunt the same houses and spaces year after year? Some people believe that they are locked in a time warp and can be seen by those who are sensitive to such things. I do not believe this. What I do believe is that part of their *mind* is in a time warp. In a dimensional time warp they would be trapped all the time, unable to escape. In that of the mind, however, they would only be visiting this dimension when a particular memory, perhaps the date when a tragedy occurred, would take over their mind completely, thus projecting them for a short while into this dimension.

For example, all of us at some time or another have awful nightmares – and often it can be a memory of the past that would be better forgotten. This is taking place whilst you are asleep, when your mind partially leaves the body and links with another dimension.

Of course, this is a simple explanation but in my experience, simple explanations are often the best. Adding unnecessary complications can mean that the magic disappears from your life. Always keep the magic – without it we have no future.

Mediums can and do release ghosts from their terrible memories by asking them to seek the light. What does this mean? When death occurs, the mind is drawn into a vortex which connects the dimensions, rather like spinning through a tunnel. This experience has been recounted repeatedly by people from all over the world when they have had a near-death experience. At the end of the tunnel there is a bright light, which signifies that you have arrived at your destination. There you will be looked after by family and friends in the spirit world, until you have recovered from the experience. Again, if you reverse this, it is similar to travelling down the birthcanal and arriving in a room where people want to give you love and care for you when you are born.

When visiting their old haunts, many ghosts become annoyed at finding someone in a bed in *their* room, and may bend over that person to get a closer look. Because of the cold induced by the ghost, the sleeping person invariably wakes up – and more often than not screams at the top of their voice. The ghost, frightened out of its wits, disappears. Well, wouldn't you?

I write books because I want everyone to have the knowledge that these experiences are to be relished. They are not an everyday occurence, and so should be enjoyed.

I am often asked why it is that the people who are the most frightened of ghosts and visions should see them, and those who would really love to see them don't.

Again, there is a simple answer. When you are over-sensitive, as most people are who dread seeing ghosts, then your energies are always heightened and the mind energy expands, linking into the energy dimension which the ghost is inhabiting. If you see a ghost, then you are partly invading their world as they are ours. It is a simple mind-to-mind contact. When they realize that you have seen them, they are as surprised as you.

One weekend I decided to have a break at an old manor house, that is now an inn. It was quiet and peaceful, and I thought it would be nice to lie on the bed in the afternoon and relax. I went to sleep. Suddenly, I woke with a start to see the ghost of a young girl bending over me. I call her a ghost because her clothes were so old-fashioned. I smiled at her but she continued to look puzzled, as though I shouldn't have been there at all. After about five minutes she disappeared. I was very excited by this and told my husband about it as soon as he returned.

About eighteen months later, I happened to choose the same inn for fortnightly workshops. Whilst I was making all the arrangements with the manager I asked him if he knew they had a ghost. 'Why do you say that?' he asked. I smiled, and explained what had happened on my last visit. I described the clothes the young girl was wearing. He laughed, and asked which room I had stayed in. When I told him he said, 'Yes, that was Elizabeth's room, and it is now named after her. She died tragically many years ago, when this was still a family home.' He then told me the story. Apparently, she had been very much in love with a young man who lived in a house nearby, but they had been forbidden to see each other. Consequently, they used to meet in a tunnel which connected the two houses.

Unfortunately, during one of these clandestine meetings, the tunnel caved in and buried them. The manager looked at me. 'Perhaps we should make more of our ghost,' he said. 'We might attract more visitors.'

There are many people who love to stay in old haunted houses, hotels or inns, and yet will run a mile from a modern establishment with a ghost or spirit.

I was staying with Alan, my husband, in a well-known London hotel. The room was warm and comfortable and the atmosphere relaxing. We had dinner, then retired early. I was woken at about 3 a.m. by the sound of ice cubes being shaken, and saw a spirit standing by the ice-bucket in the corner of the room. He said, 'Will you help me? I died of a heart attack in this hotel three years ago.'

He looked very distressed, and I promised to help if I could. Just before he disappeared, I woke my husband and asked him if he could see the spirit. He couldn't see anything at all. After a while we both went back to sleep, and slept soundly for the rest of the night.

In the morning, I sought out a friend of mine who worked at the hotel, and told her the story. She couldn't believe it. According to her, no-one else had ever seen this spirit, so it was obviously his first appearance. This often happens when a medium visits a haunted place. The spirits are aware that you are going to be there, and make sure they put in an appearance so that they can be recognized and understood. My friend promised to speak to the security guard who had been working at the hotel for about four years. 'He would know whether anyone had died of a heart attack in that time,' she said.

We were walking through the foyer after breakfast when my friend called me over and told me that she had spoken with the security guard. Apparently he had gone as white as a sheet. She explained that up until now he had always thought stories of the paranormal to be absolute rubbish, and said that she had never seen him so disturbed. He wanted to see me. I went to meet him in the restaurant. He was in his thirties, and did not look the type of man to be easily frightened. We had a cup of tea together. 'My God!' he said. 'You've frightened the life out of me. I have never believed in ghosts or spirits before.' He really did look upset. 'Why should you believe me now?' I asked. He leaned forward, resting his face on his hands. 'I believe you because the story you are telling is the truth – and nobody but myself knows about it. The rest of the staff change all the time. I've been here longer than any of them.' Then he confided in me. 'A man died in his bath about three years ago, and I had to get him out. It was a really unpleasant experience. What's more, it was on the same floor that you are occupying at the moment – the room is only four doors away, in fact.' I asked if anyone else had died of a heart attack during the last three or four years. 'No, he is the only one,' he said. We sat for about half-an-hour, whilst I explained a few simple psychic facts and promised to give him a copy of *Mind to Mind* so that he could have a better understanding of the subject. He thanked me, then said, 'The really unbelievable thing about this is that he died three years ago to this month.' Then he left to continue with his duties, looking really bewildered. I felt rather sorry for him. The news spread around the hotel like wildfire. By lunchtime I had been inundated with enquiries from the staff, who were fascinated and frightened at the same time.

When I walked into the restaurant for dinner it was obvious that all the staff had been informed. The restaurant manager was particularly interested and wanted to hear more.

As I was settling down for the second night, I hoped I wouldn't have another visit. Alas, it was not to be. I awoke at about the same time to the sound of ice cubes being stirred. This man had obviously liked his drink! He looked as though he were in his late forties, had dark hair, and was quite good-looking. His image was much clearer than the previous night. He told me that he hadn't had time to say goodbye to his daughters, and wanted to speak to them. Then he gave me part of an address and disappeared.

I sought out the security guard the next morning and asked him to have breakfast with me. I told him that the same spirit had visited me again. He looked at me. 'I hope you're joking,' he said. I assured him that I was not, and gave him the rest of the message. I also gave him the address I had been given, even though it wasn't complete. 'I know that's correct,' he said, 'because I had to contact their aunt, and I remember the location.' He kept shaking his head. 'I really cannot believe this. Everything you have told me is absolutely true, but I'm the only one who knows the whole story. I must admit, Betty, I think I am beginning to believe in this sort of thing. I could not have had more convincing evidence.' He told me that the man had been forty-eight years of age, was divorced, but had two daughters from the marriage. He had moved abroad and was about to get married again, but had returned to England on a visit. His two daughters had actually been waiting for him in the restaurant. When he was over an hour late, they asked the security guard if they could look in his room. He agreed, and accompanied them upstairs. When he opened the door, he found the father dead in the bath. He ushered the girls out and found someone to look after them whilst he arranged for the body to be removed.

When he had finished telling me the full story, he shook his head. 'I have read part of the book you gave me,' he said. 'Tell me how do you do it.' 'Do what?' I asked. 'Well, this sort of thing,' he replied. 'Being able to see and speak to spirits.' I laughed. 'As a matter of fact, they do all the talking. I just listen. I think perhaps you should read the rest of my book.' As we were about to leave the restaurant, I asked him if he was going to do anything about the spirit visitor. 'What can I do?' he asked. I suggested that he get in touch with the aunt. Perhaps she could pass on the messages I had received to the daughters. He thought about this, and promised to see what he could do. He was going to have to ask permission from the management, because all the files were confidential. We said goodbye, and I told him not to worry about the situation. He was a very conscientious person, and his loyalties had to be with his employers. The management are great friends of mine, and I had no wish to upset them.

When the news of the latest developments were passed on, the hotel was once again buzzing with excitement. I had to leave for an appointment, and the hotel was quiet when I returned, so Alan and I were able to leave peacefully.

I thought the incident would be quickly forgotten. I myself had put it out of my mind within hours of returning home. However, this was not to be.

I had to return to the same hotel some three weeks later, as I was appearing on television the following day. My friend was waiting for me when I arrived, and told me that the manager would like to have tea with me.

He was extremely nice, and said that it was a pleasure to see me again – although later I was not so sure that he had really meant it – and I wondered what on earth I could do for him. He said, 'Betty, if you see anything in your room tonight would you keep it to yourself? I am rather worried about my guests. If they hear these stories, nobody will want to sleep on that particular floor.'

He told me that he had given me a suite on the top floor, right away from the floor I had occupied previously. He was obviously not going to take any chances.

As it happened, I did not see any more spirits, but that did not prevent the staff on the following morning, enquiring whether I had slept well. They could not wait for the next instalment.

In this New Age there are more psychic children than ever before. They are more aware than their parents.

Raina, my granddaughter who is now ten, has seen spirits from the age of two, just as I did. Only recently, she

98

was standing behind the front door of her home, and suddenly said to her mother, 'Look, I can see all this swirling mist over the door.' As she became more excited she told her mother that it was beginning to spiral and that it was beautiful. Janet said the little girl's face was a picture as she absorbed the wonder of it. Raina wanted to know what it was. Janet told her that because they had been looking at a scary picture on television and were frightened, the spirits had come to calm them down. Because she had already seen spirits herself, Raina accepted this explanation. Since that day her life has been so much easier, and she is accomplishing more than she or Janet ever dreamed.

It is so rewarding to know that someone is looking after you.

I remember a client telling me about her son, who was drowned at sea in 1942. She had been fast asleep, and woke with a start. The room was icy, and she could see her son standing at the foot of the bed. He was as white as a sheet, and looked really dejected. At first she thought he had shore leave and was ill but, as she was about to get out of bed to hug him, he disappeared into the floor. She screamed at the top of her voice, waking the whole house. When asked by her daughter what had happened, she just said, 'Tommy's dead.' The daughter sat and listened to the story but was convinced her mother had only been dreaming. About a week later, the mother received a telegram to say that her son's ship had gone down with all hands. He had visited her to say goodbye.

There had been so many similar stories, reported by many people who were unaware at the time that an afterlife existed, that I am completely amazed when intelligent people still question it. Scientists continue to be sceptical about the whole thing and until they can recapture the child within, they will always be out of touch with the true reality.

People have seen me standing by their bedsides whilst I myself was sleeping – and someone in the energy dimension has probably wondered why I, a complete stranger, am wandering around in their particular patch.

During my travels by car around the country I often pass through a town or village that 'gives me the creeps'. I was speaking to a friend one day about a particular village, when she mentioned that she had owned a shop in that same village. She told me that she had hated it, and had been relieved when it was sold. She went on to tell me this story.

'Whilst I still owned the shop, my father visited me, as he was interested in the adjoining property. When he returned from viewing the property, he said that he had been talking to a little old lady who lived in the cottage around the corner to the shop. I told him I had never met her. He was surprised, and gave me a graphic description of her. I must admit I was puzzled, because it was a very tight knit community. Why hadn't she been in the shop before if it was only around the corner?

'Then, one day, about a year after this conversation had taken place, I was serving in the shop when a little old lady walked in. She had something wrong with her leg, and looked very frail. Her clothes were old-fashioned, and she wore a headscarf. She bought a loaf of bread, but because she looked so frail I offered to lock up the shop and run her home. I turned to get my keys and followed her to the door, where she vanished from my sight. I could not believe it. Thinking about it later, I remembered the description of the old lady given to me by my father. It was the same person.'

Something obviously triggered the old lady's memory to

make her return annually. And it was quite probable that she used to buy goods in the little shop when she was alive.

I hope I have convinced you that there is nothing to worry about should you ever see a ghost or a spirit.

Poltergeists, however are quite something else. Read on.

9

Poltergeists

The word poltergeist is derived from the combination of
two German words, *polter* – noisy, and *geist* – spirit.

The evidence for the existence of poltergeists is overwhelming. Cases have been studied by physicists, scientists, parapsychologists, mediums and technical experts of
all kinds, and they have all been baffled. All have had their
theories, but none have yet come up with an answer to the
phenomenon.

Poltergeist activity consists of objects being thrown
across the room. Light bulbs burst, cupboards move,
pictures fall off walls, chairs are knocked over, and water
invariably makes an appearance, either on the floor or the
carpet. Practically anything can be hurled around when
this kind of spirit is loose.

Because many poltergeists make their appearance when
there are children in the house, it would be easy to assume
that they are mischievous spirit children. But this is not
always the case.

When I returned to England after living in Spain for
many years, I lived with my husband and daughter in a
rented flat. It belonged to a clergyman, and we were asked
not to have anything to do with the occult whilst we were
in residence. We agreed – we had more urgent matters to
attend to – but I thought the request was surprising. At
this time I had no idea of my mediumistic gifts, although I

had given hand analysis to my friends for many years. Nevertheless, our landlord knew nothing about me.

One day whilst we were having a meal there was a crash from the bedroom. We hurried into the room, and there in front of us was the door of a very heavy wardrobe. It had been taken off its hinges and dropped on the floor.

Living in the flat became irksome. There were disturbances day and night, and it became obvious to me that the clergyman had been well aware of these activities. His request was now understandable. It seemed unlikely that the flat had been exorcised. If it had been, it certainly hadn't done much good. We were surrounded by noisy spirits, and they were not going to leave.

I must say it did not bother us very much when we were together, but being left alone in the flat was another matter. This phenomenon is a nuisance to all who come into contact with it.

One theory about the existence of poltergeists is that the hormonal activity in children at the time of puberty creates some sort of magnetic disturbance that draws objects towards them. The same explanation is given about women of menopausal age – and, as it happens, these are the age groups that are most often affected. Unfortunately, people who are at other stages of their lives can also be affected by this problem.

Close friends of mine once lived in a house that had a poltergeist, although it was not active until there were people in the house that it did not like. Then all the tools that were stacked behind an old stove were thrown to the floor. It was some time before my friends realized that the spirit was trying to warn them against these particular people – and in each case they found they could not entirely trust them.

After a while, they found it comforting to know that

someone was looking after their interests, and when they moved house they sorely missed their poltergeist.

Another theory is that there is some sort of centrifugal force that whirls things around, but this has to be discounted because the objects are usually aimed at one particular person.

There appears to be an intelligence behind all the actions, and I believe that in all these cases there is a mind-to-mind contact. Everyone has their own unique vibrational mind waves. If two opposing vibrational mind waves meet head on, then that can cause a tremendous power conflict. If the mind of the dead person is more powerful than that of the living, then you have a poltergeist.

Many children can actually see the spirit involved, and when they describe it, especially if the spirit is a child, they are usually scolded for having too vivid an imagination.

How many parents, I wonder, have been asked by their children to lay another place at the table for a spirit friend – or have seen their children talking to someone who, to them, is invisible? There must be hundreds – I have heard so many of these stories myself.

It is not necessarily only psychic children that see spirit children. The stories that I have heard are, in many cases, about children with no obvious psychic ability. Noisy spirit children are attracted like to like, and there we have the collision of minds.

It has also been noted that poltergeist activity begins when someone makes it quite obvious that they are sceptical about spirits.

This story was told to me by a client. A woman friend in her late seventies lost her husband, and whilst my client was arranging flowers in the local church for his funeral, the widow walked in and declared that it was all a waste of time as there was no such thing as an afterlife.

Several days later, the widow's house was bombarded with stones. The police were called, and they searched all the waste ground behind the house and watched it day and night.

They could not find any culprits, but the stones continued to fall. This went on for months. My client was there one day whilst it was happening, and was amazed to see that the stones fell softly and did not move after they touched the earth.

The roof of the house was extremely high, and yet the stones sailed right over. If they had been thrown from any distance, they would never have reached that height.

The police, fed up with their fruitless search over many months, flew a helicopter over the area. Still the culprit was not found.

Eventually, it stopped of its own accord. I believe the dead woman's husband was furious with her for stating that there was no afterlife, especially if he had been reborn. Why do I think my theory is correct? The timing. There was nothing amiss until the widow denounced the afterlife.

Hundreds of sceptics have experienced phenomena of some kind when they, too, have dismissed life after death. They cannot all be coincidences.

It is true that poltergeist activity is rare, but it is only one of the many unpleasant phenomena that such sceptics have witnessed. At a party one evening a very unpleasant man was giving forth about idiots who believed in the occult and especially the afterlife. Thoroughly enjoying the spotlight, he continued his ranting for an hour. Suddenly, a wine glass hit him on the head giving him a nasty gash. Everyone looked round and stared in the direction from which the glass had apparently been aimed. The space was empty and there was no exit.

After the man had left, the hosts discussed this extraordinary happening with the remaining guests. There was no doubt at all they were all quite shocked, and they all swore they were not the culprits. I knew them all intimately, and it was obvious they were speaking the truth.

There is a man, known to a friend of mine, who is violently sick every time he dismisses survival after death. One could say that it is a psychosomatic reaction, but this theory must be discounted as he had no idea it was going to happen the first time and did not expect it to happen again. Perhaps it was a poltergeist turning on the heat. After all, to have people dismiss the afterlife must be extremely upsetting to spirits. It is no different to denying the existence of people in this dimension.

There is another theory which seems to have some substance, and that is that sick people attract these noisy spirits. Sickness begins in the energy counterpart and mind about eighteen months before it manifests on the physical body. During this time, the energy is gradually being depleted and that person's regular exercise programme diminishes. Anxiety stimulates the adrenalin glands and they produce an abundance of adrenalin which is an acid hormone. This floods the system causing even greater havoc, and is responsible for the build-up of static electricity. In turn, this can have the magnetic effect of attracting objects towards that person.

To prevent this happening put your hands under cold running water for a few minutes twice a day – more if you still feel 'electric'.

There is an answer to the problems caused by poltergeists and that is to work on your own mind by not harbouring bad thoughts towards others. Remember, like always attracts like, and by cleaning up our own act we can avoid being pestered by unwanted spirits of any sort.

Fear of anything is our greatest enemy. Whether it is from this life or the next, if a particular type of personality knows you are afraid of them they will pursue. Your greatest weapon against this kind of nightmare is the power of your own mind. Professional mediums rarely have poltergeist problems. I believe this is due to the fact that they 'know' protection is given to them because of their spiritual contacts.

Before you leave this chapter let me remind you that poltergeists are quite rare and there is no need to worry about them. The most important exercise you can do is to work on your mind waves and always send out loving thoughts; love is the most powerful energy of all.

10

Thought Projection or Genuine Psychic Photography

Thoughts are energy – mind energy – and it is possible to project a thought so that it appears on a photograph. It is also possible for thoughts that are *not* projected to appear on photographs.

I have seen photographs of mediums surrounded by many well-known spirit people. It is extremely difficult for amateur or professional to say whether these are really spirits or thought-forms. The arguments have been going on for years as to whether one person or another is a fraud.

For me, the intriguing thing about it is that whether thought-form or genuine spirit, both types of manifestation are due to mind waves. This seems to have been overlooked by psychic researchers. Here we have incredible phenomena occurring, and they refuse to see it, so carried away are they in trying to prove someone is being fraudulent. This, alas, is the case with most psychical research.

I have actually seen thought-forms when giving trance healing. I remember my first experience.

I was sitting by the side of the healing couch with my hands on the head of a little boy and his mother was sitting opposite me in an armchair. Whilst in trance, I was aware of small clouds of energy emanating from around her head. The image of a little girl was formed from one of the clouds. It was quite distinct.

When I came out of trance, I noticed that the woman was half-asleep. I touched her arm and told her that I had finished healing. Then I asked her whether she had been dreaming. 'No,' she replied, 'I wasn't really asleep, just day-dreaming, and wondering whether my friend had picked my daughter up from school on time.' She continued, 'I always worry myself sick when I can't pick her up myself because I never really trust other people to drive carefully.'

I decided to tell her what I had seen, and described the little girl I had seen formed out of the energy. To say that she was amazed would be an understatement. She told me that I had accurately described her daughter.

I told her that this had been my first experience of this particular phenomenon, and we sat and talked about it for some time.

The next time she brought her son for healing she decided, without telling me, that she would deliberately think about her daughter again. When I had finished the healing session she asked if I had seen anything this time. My answer had to be a definite 'No'.

'Well, I tried really hard to think of my daughter. I thought you would be able to see it,' she said.

At the time, I did not understand it and had no answer. Now of course, after many years of studying and harnessing energy, I know that the more effort that is put into any thought projection the less effect it will have. In fact, it causes a block. This is because one is harnessing too much energy, and it congests.

I now also understand that thought projection from a physical person is a part of the subconscious, and thought projection from a spirit person is part of a higher consciousness.

How do I know this? The energy is quite different. With thought transference, it seems to be a heavier energy that takes time to form. It also emerges from a spot below the top of the head – in other words, the part of the mind energy that is partly submerged into the physical body.

When the energy is a mind projection from a spirit person, it is fluid and forms almost instantaneously. The forms are more complicated and distinctive.

The little boy's mother had found the key and opened the door subconsciously. Unfortunately, she closed it again – changing the pattern – by putting a lot of physical effort into it. As far as I know, she never found the key again.

There must be hundreds of us who have found keys and lost them again in this way – so be warned.

On another occasion I was sitting in a room with a friend. It was dusk, but neither of us wished to turn the light on as we were feeling extremely relaxed. Something caught my attention. A small cloud of energy, emanating from my friend, was taking on the form of a small dog. It was impossible to ascertain the real colour but I had a mind impression of it being black and white.

I asked her whether she had been thinking of a dog. She replied, 'Yes! I was thinking about my little dog that died about eight years ago. We always sat in my lounge together at dusk.'

I had not previously discussed thought projection with her, and warned her not to *try* to project images as she would lose the key.

It would be a real breakthrough if one could photograph spirits whilst receiving communication from them. Just imagine being able to see loved family and friends again, and having positive proof in the form of a photograph.

Unfortunately, like all psychic phenomena, this nearly always occurs spontaneously. Very rarely does one receive messages in advance of something spectacular happening. I might perhaps receive a message giving me an idea that something will happen, but it is usually only about an hour beforehand. That is why most so-called scientific experiments into this phenomenon cannot work.

Photographs taken of myself many years ago invariably had a column of light through them. Sometimes there were two columns. At the time I had no idea of the cause. I do not know even to this day whether it was energy that had not formed into a spirit, or whether it was healing energy.

In one photograph, taken after I had become a professional medium, there was an image of someone but it was very indistinct.

The photographs that are taken of me today do not have anything untoward on them. I believe this is due to the fact that my energy is used all the time with absent healing, contact healing and healing through the written word.

I have had my photograph taken many times whilst healing to try to catch a spirit doctor or two. I'm afraid it did not work. Perhaps I should have asked their permission?

There have been many mediums who have been able to hold a film and impress a picture upon it without the use of a camera. There have been others who have strapped a film to their forehead, and a spirit person or persons have left a picture of themselves on the film.

I believe that there will be a breakthrough in the future and that spirit photography will become almost an everyday occurrence.

There certainly is a vast amount of evidence to show that spirits have been captured on photographs. Especially by Hans Holzer. He studied archaeology and history at the University of Vienna and at Columbia University. He has been active as a specialist in the study and interpretation of parapsychology.

In his book *Psychic Photography: Threshold of a New Science?* he has extremely interesting photographs showing spirits and thought-forms. But mostly spirits. He gives information of how and when these photographs were taken. Time, place, light conditions, camera, film, operator, developing. If he was not operating the camera himself, he observed those who were. Checking all the time.

Although this book was published in 1969 it is worth acquiring if you wish to make a study of spirit photography – if only for the precision with which he carried out his investigations.

I have often wished that I had carried a small camera around with me when I have visited old houses and inns, especially when I have felt something brush past me on a staircase or in a long corridor. Perhaps I could have photographed something that I could not see at that time.

If this chapter has interested you, why not experiment with a camera at home, or, even better, in a place that is known to be haunted. You do not necessarily have to be a medium yourself or to have one present. You may find that you have natural mediumistic abilities and are able to attract spirits. There is only one way to find out. Just do it.

11

Remote Viewing

When I was evacuated from London at the beginning of
the war, I spent many lonely hours by myself. My friends
lived in isolated farms or were miles away in other villages.
It was at this time that I practised remote viewing for the
first time, although, of course, I had no idea at that time
that I was doing anything unusual.

I remember my first attempt. I was feeling very
unhappy and thought that I would close my eyes and visit
my home in London to see if I could locate my mother. I
found myself at the beginning of our road, and started to
walk up it. I reached the house and opened the gate,
closing it behind me, and then I looked at the lilac tree,
which was always so beautiful in summer. It looked bare
and forlorn. Well, it was a cold and miserable November
day. I peered through the glass panel in the door, and
knocked. The door opened and I walked down the
corridor to the kitchen. I smelt the aroma of fairy cakes
which filled me with delight. I sat down in front of the fire
with tea and cakes; it was wonderful. Then the vision
vanished, I opened my eyes and I was alone again. I
wanted to go back home and I closed my eyes but nothing
happened. I was devastated.

Fortunately, I was not put off by this. I tried again the
next day, and the next, until I became proficient. I visited
all my favourite places in London, and visited my friends

often, although their faces were always quite misty, never clear. With my new ability I rarely felt lonely, I believe it was a gift to help me through those homesick years.

My mother soon moved to the area, living only a few miles away. It was then that I occasionally asked her what she had been doing at certain times of the day. She used to laugh and ask me why I wanted to know. I told her that I liked to think of her, and that sometimes I could imagine her doing certain things, like sitting and knitting. She would sometimes confirm what I had seen, while at other times she would just laugh. It didn't stop me from using my new technique. It did not matter to me whether I was right or wrong – I enjoyed the journeys and they made me feel happier.

I am quite sure psychiatrists would have had a field day with me if they had had the chance.

Eventually, my family settled in Surrey. Our house had gone – a fate we shared with thousands. We lived with relatives for a while, then settled in a home of our own.

I had always been called a dreamer by my family and I continued to dream. My other world was more real to me, and yet I have always been an earthy person, logical and certainly extremely analytical. I have always felt balanced, and I believe throughout my life that this has been proved time and again.

For years, I have listened to scientists trying to explain phenomena. In most cases their explanations seem quite pathetic. They are unable to have multi-dimensional experiences because their minds are closed. Mind energy cannot expand when answers are sought in this dimension – and they would also have to forget most of their training. Having said that, there are scientists who have been able to bridge the gap, but their number is few. This is our great loss.

My daughter, Janet, and I practised remote viewing when we lived in an isolated spot in Spain many years ago. We used to let our minds travel to the nearest village, entering bars and cafés to find out whether our friends were there. We were extremely successful. By the time we left Spain, Janet was a fully fledged remote viewer. Neither of us were mediums at that time, but I am sure that it aided our progression by understanding that the mind can and does travel. Once you have control over the mind energy and it is disciplined, becoming psychic is the next step. That is, if you wish it. Always remember *you* are in control.

Becoming telepathic will be another bonus. Because you are sending your mind energy ahead of your physical body, it will become used to reaching out. Consequently, from time to time, it will touch other people's minds. You may find yourself speaking without thinking and a person with you will comment, 'I was just going to say that!' This often happens with partners and other close relationships, and is quite common.

Mind energy can also be split, and it is possible for the personality to be in different places at the same time. I mentioned in my earlier books that I have been seen standing at the bedside of an ill person when my physical body and my conscious mind have been somewhere else. In many cases this phenomenon occurs when the sick person and I are oceans apart. Sai Baba, the Holy Man of India, has demonstrated this ability many times, appearing to as many as three or four people at a time, perhaps more. I have only managed to appear to one person at a time, and that unknowingly. Only very progressed persons such as Sai Baba can actually control this state.

I hope that I have whetted your appetite, and that you are ready to start on your first exercise. Please do keep strictly to the exercises as this will keep your mind disciplined.

Remote Viewing 1

1 Find somewhere peaceful where you know you will not be disturbed for at least ten minutes.

2 Sit down in a comfortable chair. Close your eyes and breathe deeply three times.

3 Now, mentally walk to your back door or whichever door leads to the garden. (Do not worry if you have no garden – just mentally leave your home and go to the nearest park, or to a neighbour's garden.) Open the door and walk out into the garden. Walk around slowly, looking at the trees and plants, bend down to smell the flowers if it is summer. Walk over to a tree or bush, or even the garden fence. Touch it, feel the texture. Above all, be observant. You may see things you have not seen before, and if this is so you can always check it physically later. Enjoy the experience.

4 Lie down on the lawn – or, if it is damp, put a cover down and then lie down. Keep the images going. Look up. If there is a blue cloudless sky feel yourself being drawn towards it. If there are clouds, feel yourself being carried away with them. Now mentally close your eyes and *feel* the peace.

5 Now get up and walk back to your house. Open the same door, walk through it and close it. Return to the chair and open your eyes.

If you have done this exercise correctly, you will now be feeling totally peaceful. If you do not, then you were too tense. Don't worry – it will be better next time.

If you found that you could not see anything at all, perhaps you will not feel too bad if I tell you that very few people can actually 'see' anything. You simply *know* you are there, you *know* you are looking at the trees and plants, and you *know* that you are touching the trees, bushes or fence.

It is the same as being physically blind, although in this case you are psychically blind. Television is damaging to the psyche, the picture and the storyline is there for all to see, whereas, when children or adults read books their imagination is working overtime, visualizing the scenes and the characters. These pictures last and every time you think of that book, no matter how long after you have read it, you see the same scenes and characters as your mind first imagined them.

I believe that mind expansion should be taught in schools. I cannot emphasize this strongly enough. Unless one has been taught from an early age, when the mind is more open, we must learn mind expansion when we are much older and it is much more difficult.

Remote viewing can help to counteract the damage and make up for so much that has been lost in our society.

Becoming proficient in remote viewing is a tremendous leap for you, so please do not become despondent if you are not successful at first. These exercises are a natural follow-on from the exercises in *Mind Magic*. If you have been successful with them, you will find that the effort has been worth it and you will be several steps ahead of those who have not carried out the previous exercises.

When *knowing* enters your life you will wonder how you ever did without it.

Now let us try another exercise.

Remote Viewing 2

This time you will have to ask a friend or relative's permission to enter their home and you will find it a great help if you have a tape recorder ready so that you can speak into it as you go on your journey. You can then check and re-check what you have seen.

1 Once again, find somewhere peaceful, and sit in a comfortable chair. Give yourself plenty of time for this exercise. Relax, and breathe deeply three times.

2 Visualize your mind energy straining at the leash. Now allow it the freedom to reach out and absorb cosmic forces that will strengthen and revitalize. Watch it as it expands forever outward, *ad infinitum*. Now watch as it returns to you glowing and vibrant. Mentally bring it to the shape of a halo. Again, if you cannot see anything mentally, *know* that it is happening.

3 Visualize the route to your appointed destination. Be quite sure that you know in advance what route you are going to take. You cannot change your route when you are halfway there. Are you going to walk or go by car? If you usually occupy the passenger seat, then imagine that you have your usual driver with you or perhaps a spirit driver.

4 Now prepare to leave your home. Do all the things you would normally do if you were going out. Proceed

towards the door and open it, walk through, and close it. From now on, you will be a part of your surroundings. Progress along your chosen route.

5 You have completed your journey. Walk up to the front door and ring the bell. The door will be opened. You will now find yourself in the house, walk around taking in everything that you see or *know* is there. Go all over the building; do not miss anything.

6 Now open the back door if there is one, and walk out into the garden. Try to guess the size. It does not matter at all if your guess is wrong.

7 When you have finished, make your way to the front door and leave, closing the door behind you.

8 Make your way home along the same route. Never take a different route home.

9 Open your eyes. Telephone your friend and describe what you have seen. Although you have visited their home before, things are always changing around the house, and there is bound to be something new.

10 Before you 'travel' to them again, arrange with your friend or relative that they leave something on their dining-room table. Perhaps they would like to try remote viewing themselves. This way you could both practise regularly. It is fun.

In *Mind Magic*, I introduced you to Peter Williams. He is the gentleman who has multiple sclerosis. When he and I can find the time he comes along for his 'rejuvenation', as he calls it. One day after a healing session I was telling him about remote viewing, and he challenged me to visit the house of a friend of his. I told him that he would have to obtain their permission, but he assured me that he would be given this. I asked him for the address, closed my eyes and thought about it. I described the front of the house, then opened the door and walked in.

As I entered the hall I gave a detailed description of it, the staircase and a plan of the ground floor, including its contents. I walked into the lounge, and as I was giving a description of the room I happened to look at the wall above the fireplace. On it was a picture which looked rather peculiar. It was of a lady in an old-fashioned dress, but the face looked as though it had been glued on, rather clown-like. I could not understand this at all. Peter thought I was wrong. He said that he had never seen anything like that in his friend's house. I assured him, however, that it *was* there. I then walked through the rest of the house, and went through into the dining room, describing the patio doors that led to the paved area outside. There was trellis work around the patio and beyond it was a garden about 65 feet in length. All correct. Then I went into the kitchen, and said they had just installed new pine furniture. Again all correct and Peter looked at me in amazement. I then went upstairs and gave an accurate description of the bathroom and bedrooms. In the main bedroom I saw some heated rollers on the dressing table. Shirley, Peter's wife, said, 'You are correct – I told my friend to buy them.' When I had finished, Peter said, 'I have known you all this time, and I did not realize you could do this.' I laughed. 'Peter, I do not have time to show off my party pieces all the time.' 'OK Betty,' he said, 'you've proved your point, but you're wrong about the picture.' I asked him to telephone his friend when he got home, and to ask her about it. There was definitely something odd about the face. He said he would do that.

He rang me the next day and told me that while his friend had been on holiday, she had been photographed with her head through a cut-out of an old-fashioned lady. Hence the clown-like appearance, and it had come out so well she had hung it on the wall.

This proves that with remote viewing you are not picking up the information telepathically – although according to the sceptics even that would not be possible.

I cannot emphasize enough the strength, power and potential of mind energy. Only about 8 per cent of the potential is used. It is an utter waste of a gift, something that we all have and do not know how to use.

Mind waves flow back and forth, like the sea. Always moving, seeking like minds and absorbing information. The imagination is the control. It is also the disciplinarian. A disciplined mind is a happy mind, one that knows where it is going and what it is supposed to do. Butterfly minds are those that flit from one thought to another without any control. That is a complete waste of time. There are millions of butterfly minds in this world and their potential is being completely wasted.

Remote viewing gives control and discipline back to the owner. Whether or not you are successful with these exercises, you are still disciplining your mind. No effort is wasted. *You* will be in control of your life, your emotions, and *you* will direct it from the *control tower*; in other words, the imagination.

I have used remote viewing for absent healing and on more than one occasion it has saved lives.

About three years ago I mentally visited a lady who lived in the North of England. I used to give her healing and this became a part of my everyday routine for about six weeks. One day I entered her home to find her at the bottom of the stairs, looking extremely unwell. I telephoned her daughter and described the scene, and asked if she would visit her mother who lived about six miles away. She agreed. That same evening she 'phoned to tell me that her mother had fallen down the stairs and she had been taken to hospital. Her condition was critical; had she lain there all night she could have died.

When you practise remote viewing you probably will not 'see' anything, but if there is anything wrong you will have a feeling in the pit of your stomach that something is not quite right. We are all different, and you may get your warning signs another way, but you most certainly will *feel* something. Perhaps you will be able to avert a catastrophe.

You may feel that if you have alerted someone and there turns out to be nothing wrong that you would feel silly. Forget it. When you are dealing with mind energy and you are not yet fully qualified, then you will make mistakes. And after all, it is much better to try to help than not to help at all. It may be that what you are picking up is a family quarrel, and not something that is terribly serious. Finding this out would still boost your morale. At least you are picking up *something*! Be courageous.

Are you ready for another experiment?

Remote Viewing 3

1 Find a quiet place where you will not be disturbed. Sit in a comfortable chair, close your eyes and relax. Breathe deeply three times.

2 Think of someone who is unwell. If you do not know

their address, don't worry. Simply think of their name and you will automatically be there – that is if you have carried out the previous exercises correctly.

3 You are now in their home. Picture them sitting in a comfortable chair. Now place your hands on their shoulders and ask for help in their recovery. In this healing mode you may be given some information about the illness and why they are suffering from it.

4 When you feel the healing has been successful simply think yourself back home again.

5 Wait a day or two before you make any enquiries about the health of your patient.

6 Keep whatever information you may have received to yourself. All spiritual work is confidential. Keep records to guide you; this way you can judge whether or not you are making any progress.

Remote viewing is extremely useful when you are worried about children and their whereabouts. You can scan the area in which you live, looking for them. It is useful for checking up on elderly parents to ensure they are all right.

It is also useful when used from room to room, such as offices. If your boss is in his office and you are waiting for the right time to ask for a raise, simply use remote viewing to absorb the atmosphere around him to find out whether or not it is the right time.

All the feelings you will have will be extremely subtle, and there will be many times when you are not sure what feelings you *are* getting. Again, please do not worry. With practice you will learn how to differentiate. It takes time.

Perhaps I can encourage you with the results I had with the workshops I gave every fortnight during the winter of 1991.

They were devised to take people through the exercises in *Mind Magic*, but they turned out to be so much more. In this chapter I will only relate the success we had with remote viewing. The majority of the participants had never heard of it, let alone practised it, so you can imagine the surprise when I asked them to turn around to their neighbour and ask permission to look into their handbags or wallet.

Once this permission had been given, I asked them to relax and close their eyes, and simply allow their mind energy to mentally open the handbag or wallet as though they were physically carrying out this operation. The next thing was to look into the bag or wallet and really rummage around, trying to find something that was significant. When they had finished, I asked them to open their eyes and tell their partner what they had seen.

The findings were hilarious, and there was much laughter as objects which had been correctly identified were taken from their bag or wallet by the owner and displayed.

It was also an interesting experiment, in so far as it made obvious the fact that the energy of an object remains after it has ceased to be in the holder. One lady said that she could see a fresh rose inside a handbag. In fact, the rose had been there the previous day but was not in the handbag at the time. I have known of this phenomenon for years, but most of the people participating in the afternoon's experiment had not even heard of it until then.

Remote viewing is fun. Try it, and good luck.

12

Psychokinesis and Metal Bending

There are many psychics who use the power of their mind to move objects. This is called psychokinesis.

The Russians lead the field in this direction. Many of their psychics have passed tests, such as moving the needle of a compass defying the earth's magnetic field, stopping the heart of a frog, moving objects under glass, levitating heavy objects and causing burns to appear on human flesh.

I have tried moving objects with my mind, but have never been successful. I am sure the reason for my failure lies in the fact that I feel it is a total waste of energy and time, and so subconsciously I block myself.

I still find it fascinating however, to watch those that have this gift. A friend of mine could move many objects with his mind power. The heavier the object was, the longer it took.

I asked him what his thoughts were as he carried out these exercises. He told me that he just visualized energy building up under the object until it moved, and then he guided it in the direction he wanted it to go. I must admit, the objects moved very fast once they got started.

I suggested that he tried healing so that I could check the results. He agreed, but gave up after only two weeks. He told me that he just did not have the compassion needed to heal. This confirmed what I had suspected – it wasn't a healing energy.

There are so many doors of the mind, and the keys are there if we can only find them. One has to have an open mind.

Metal bending is now quite common. Uri Geller, of course, is the man that brought it into our homes, affecting clocks, watches, spoons, forks and other objects. When he appeared on television, these things twisted and bent as though they were putty, many of them in the hands of children. This was a typical example of the collective unconscious at work. The mind waves of Uri and his audience were as one, linking into each other. Let me explain.

If a television audience is asked to link into a person with a particular gift at a certain time, then all their mind waves are being projected to that one person. His mind waves are picked up by millions of people, and they become part of a collective energy. This kind of power is quite phenomenal – hence the distorted and broken objects in all of these homes.

I have been successful with metal bending, but I do not like the feeling of the energy that is used to obtain these results. Scientists have actually felt rather ill whilst watching demonstrations of metal bending, and I believe that the energy used is destructive.

I have kept this chapter short because I feel that these occupations, though interesting, have no value. However, mind waves *are* involved, so I felt it my duty to include it in this book.

This is only my opinion, and I am sure that it will not stop people experimenting, which is how it should be.

The whole of life is an experiment. Enjoy it.

13

Dowsing

Dowsing is used by psychics and non-psychics alike. Indeed, many dowsers can become extremely irritated by the suggestion that they may be psychic – perhaps because they do not understand how they receive their information.

A dowser has to have the ability to project their mind. Whether it is map dowsing, finding lost property, or finding water, the technique is the same.

Healers use their hands as dowsing instruments, but in fact one can eventually discard 'tools' and simply use the mind.

How does it work? Let us take water divining, with hazel twigs or even a bent coat hanger. It doesn't really matter what is used as long as the diviner believes in the tools he is using. Knowing that the tools are going to work is the answer to finding anything. Once one has total faith, then it will work.

I once accompanied a friend when he was water divining. He held some hazel twigs, and we set off across the field. Suddenly the twig twisted in a downward direction. 'There's water here,' he said excitedly. Taking his spade out of a sack, he dug a hole about three feet deep, and water did indeed start to trickle into it.

Later that day he said, 'I knew I would find water there today.' When I questioned him, he told me that he was very familiar with that particular field, as he used to keep his own horses there.

What had happened here was that he had projected his mind towards the field whilst he was still at home, concentrating on it below ground level. As matter does not block energy, the mind waves entered the ground and picked up the source of water. When he actually walked around the field, he knew, subconsciously, exactly where he was going.

In this particular case a mechanical digger was brought in, and the trickle became a small pond – an invaluable asset to the farmer.

The higher mind can also seek and find ley lines, which are energy lines in the earth, similar to the meridian lines in the energy counterpart of the physical body. (I have written at great length about these in *Mind Magic*.)

I believe these energy lines are mirror images of the electro-magnetic network that surrounds this planet, and I also believe that they can be damaged by the collective unconscious mind. The damage to our environment and the heartbreak it causes to everyone affects our souls, and in turn, our total spirituality. No-one can escape.

Dowsers use these lines in a very positive way, but they can return in a few months' time to find that the ley lines have been distorted and twisted. However, they can be healed and straightened by a powerful, spiritually inclined dowser.

Many years ago, ley lines seemed to link sacred sites, medieval churches and the sites of pre-Christian religions. As people were natural psychics at this time, they probably linked into the energy network around the earth and unconsciously built their churches where the energy points were strongest. These points are called nodes.

So it is that water diviners have a natural instinct for finding ley lines, eventually becoming part of the system themselves. We are all energy beings and leave something of ourselves behind wherever we practice mind power.

I have used maps for dowsing for many years, and it is possible to find lost people, animals, cars, etc., in this way. I have also been able to give information on different areas when friends have wanted to move house. This can be very helpful.

One friend had actually decided to move to a particular area, and was going to put a deposit on a house the next day. I took out an ordinary map and dowsed the area. I didn't like the feeling at all, so I suggested that we tour in the car the following day, before she did anything drastic like signing a contract.

Whilst we were scanning the area and asking questions in shops, pubs and police stations, I still had an uneasy feeling, although on the surface everything seemed to be all right. Then we met a woman walking her three dogs in the local beauty spot. After talking to her for several minutes, we noticed a peculiar smell and asked her if she knew what it was. 'That's the dump at the back of the woods. It's continually smouldering, and the whole area suffers from the smell, depending on the direction of the wind. We've been trying to have it moved elsewhere, but to no avail. It completely ruins this area.'

Needless to say, my friend did not buy the house.

The feeling of unease I had is a very familiar one, and yet in an instance such as this, it was very difficult to pin-point the actual cause. If you have these instinctive feelings, make sure you always follow them up and establish the reason for them – they are usually correct.

As with astral travel, remote viewing and absent healing, I was able to project my mind to that particular area and become aware of the essence of the place. The uneasy feeling I received was immediate, as are all the feelings one receives psychically.

I have also dowsed maps to find possible murder victims, sometimes successfully. The problem with this type of dowsing is that the ley lines can be damaged due to the violence that has taken place, so one can only identify the area and not pin-point the exact location.

Map dowsing is very accurate when used to find lost property. Many years ago, I was asked to find a valuable sapphire and diamond ring. I obtained a plan of the house, as it was impossible for me to visit. I held my dowsing instrument over the plan, going from room to room. All the reactions were negative until I absent-mindedly began to draw floorboards on one of the rooms. I then knew instinctively that the ring had dropped through the floorboards of this room, which happened to be the owner's bedroom. I gave her this information, but she said it was impossible as the room had wall-to-wall carpeting. I nevertheless asked her to look very carefully and call me with the result.

A few hours later she rang to say that the ring had indeed been under the floorboards. Apparently, it had fallen off a pedestal basin in the room and had slipped into a hole in the carpet, where the water pipes were connected. It was only just below floor level, and so had been easy to find.

This was a typical example of allowing my mind waves to work of their own accord. Because I had more or less given up and was just day-dreaming, all blocks were removed and the information was received instinctively.

I cannot mention too often how we block our instincts with too much concentrated thought. The less impetus given to thought, the more efficient it will be.

I have been asked many times to help with the removal of wild animals from homes and farms, particularly in Africa, and to direct them to a safe haven. The owners had no wish to kill these creatures, but simply to be rid of them for their own safety. I have been able to do this successfully on a number of occasions. At one time I directed wild dogs to a place hundreds of miles away from a homestead. Two years later, the people I had helped contacted me and told me that the dogs were in their designated place and seemed to be extremely healthy.

Like many other dowsers, I have also held a dowsing instrument over the abdomen of a pregnant woman to find out the sex of the unborn child. I used this method whilst in my teenage years. Nowadays, I acquire this information with the mind, with about 95 per cent accuracy.

It only takes a split second for the information to be picked up at mind level and received in the brain/physical level. That is why the answers are so spontaneous.

Colour dowsing is something in which everyone can participate. Try this simple exercise.

Dowsing

1 Choose a pendant that you have worn often, and put it on a chain, or a piece of thin string or cotton. If you haven't a pendant, use an earring or similar piece of jewellery.

2 Take several garments of different colours out of your wardrobe. Anything will do – gloves, hats, scarves – provided that they are your property.

3 Now, take your dowsing instrument and wind the

chain around your finger until there is about six inches left to swing. Hold this over a colour that you know improves your sense of well-being when you are wearing it. Close your eyes and relax, and ask the instrument if this colour is good for you. Wait for a few moments, and then open your eyes and take note of the way the instrument is swinging. It may be describing a circle, clockwise or anti-clockwise, or just swinging in a straight line. Whatever it is, that is your positive pattern, and will be your 'Yes' answer to questions. The opposite swing will be your negative answer.

4 Now try this exercise on all the colours, and take the strongest, positive swing to indicate those colours that would be self-healing and an aid to your self-esteem.

Do not do this exercise whilst in a depressed state of mind, but wait until you are feeling happy and relaxed. Then you will have a true reading.

Of course, this is a very simple way of dowsing, but it can be helpful, and who knows, it may lead you on to more advanced techniques which can be as fascinating.

Many healers use dowsing to receive a diagnosis. They may use an instrument or their hands. I used an instrument for a short time, but received a much quicker diagnosis using the mind. It doesn't really matter, as long as the diagnosis is on the energy level and not the physical level. Finding negative congestive energy and removing it with healing very often removes the physical complaint, but for obvious reasons, a healer should never give a medical diagnosis.

If you are really interested in dowsing, there are many societies that you can join where you will meet people who will help you to understand the art. There are also shops that sell a variety of dowsing instruments.

What better way can there be to probe the hidden depths of the earth? It is only too willing to give up its secrets to those who are interested. Happy dowsing.

14

Warnings

I have received many warnings of accidents. One of these occurred whilst I was driving across the middle of France with my first husband. I suddenly informed him that our son, Geoffrey, had been involved in an accident in England.

Although I was a singer at this time, my husband was well aware of my psychic gifts and accepted them. As a result we were both very agitated, and it spoilt the rest of our holiday, especially as Geoffrey was not on the phone and we could not contact him. I was sure he was badly injured.

I knew that there had been some kind of crash because I felt the impact when I received the warning. It was almost as though I had been involved myself.

When we arrived home we found Geoffrey fit and well, but his motorbike and sidecar had been very badly damaged. He had allowed a friend to borrow it, and it was he who was badly injured and lying in hospital.

A radio which had been a gift from my mother, and which was something I treasured, had been in the sidecar. Because I used the radio every day, my mind waves had obviously impregnated it, and I believe it was this link that sent the warning. (You will read more about this type of link in the chapter on Secrets of Inanimate Objects.)

On another occasion, I became very agitated whilst I was at home. It was one of those very rare times when

I had a free day, and I had planned to relax with a book. This was not to be. As the morning passed, the agitation became very pronounced and I knew that something awful was going to happen. At about midday I knew that there had been a car accident, and that my closest friend had been involved.

I phoned her office, and her secretary said that she was waiting for her to return as she had gone out for an early lunch. I told the secretary to phone the nearest hospital as I knew my friend would be there. She did this, and was told that my friend had just been admitted into the casualty ward.

When I am travelling in a car, my mind waves are always detecting obstacles around corners. I instinctively know when I should slow down and proceed with caution. The same thing can happen when I am following a car – I know from the prickling on the back of my neck when the driver is about to do something dangerous.

I am sure that everyone reading this chapter has had the same instinctive feelings, and they are always connected with mind waves.

On one occasion I was giving a party, and had instructed everyone to put their coats on a bed upstairs. I thought I had directed them to my bedroom. During the evening I felt as though I was suffocating, and immediately connected this feeling with my daughter Janet, who at that time was only a small child. I rushed upstairs to her room but couldn't find her. All the coats had been piled up on her bed and she was buried beneath them. She had a habit of sleeping under the bedclothes and the first person to place their coat on the bed hadn't seen her. The others had followed suit. I frantically pulled the coats off. She was sleeping peacefully, but the situation could have been dangerous had I not been warned.

On another visit to France, I went for a swim in the sea. As I was getting out of the water I had a mind message telling me that I had caught a virus from the sea water. When I repeated this to my husband he told me not to be stupid. As we had only just arrived I think he could see his longed-for holiday disappearing.

Three days later I was terribly ill, and he drove night and day to get me back to England. I was coughing all the way and felt as though I was going to die. When we got home, we called our doctor and he confirmed that my lungs had been affected by a virus. I was ill for two months.

I have been in a number of situations where I have been warned to leave buildings, and on three occasions this has saved my life, two of them during the war when I was a teenager working in London.

I am sure thousands of people all over the world receive precognitive messages. The problem with most of these messages is pin-pointing where and when the events are going to happen.

I have received messages of imminent air disasters, but have not been able to give the most vital information – time and place. Without these, the warnings are useless.

I had a warning for a client, and told her that she must alter her way of life as I believed she was in danger. About six months later she was found murdered.

If you happen to have an instinctive feeling that something is wrong and you *can* act upon it, do so. Perhaps you will also have false alarms, but unless you practise listening and acting upon your intuition you will never know how successful you can be.

There is an audible silence that is filled with information. It is only a matter of tuning in. It does help if you have a mind button to press, enabling you to tune into different wavelengths. Remember, with mind power there is no end to the tools that you can construct to help your psyche.

Once again, use your imagination and enter unknown dimensions to enhance your life.

PART THREE

THE SECRETS OF
INANIMATE
OBJECTS

15

The Secrets of Inanimate Objects

Every inanimate object and building has a tale to tell.

Secreted away in the material and structure are energies that have formed pictures and vibrations. These secrets can be tapped by anyone with psychic ability, and fortunately you need very little to be able to do it.

In all the workshops that I have taken over many years, about a third of the people present have been able, after only an hour of mind expansion, to tap the energy of an object, and give details of the owner's life.

It could be a necklace, ring, bracelet, comb or wallet. It makes no difference what it is, but it will be easier for the amateur if it has belonged just to one person.

This practice is called psychometry.

How do these pictures and vibrations become part of the object?

It will be easier to explain this if you remember that energy is capable of penetrating matter, as in the case of ghosts walking through walls.

These articles take in the mind energy of individuals and they also soak up the ethos of the whole. The more powerful the mind energies involved, the more they will block out weaker energies. Let me give you an example.

Whilst working with a group of people I asked for an object to demonstrate psychometry, and was given an antique brooch. I held it, absorbing the vibrations. The first mind picture I received was of a rather strait-laced lady, and I described her to the owner. 'That was my great-aunt, the first owner of the brooch,' she said. I then described the aunt's home, the furniture in it, and the fact that she owned a grand piano. Without warning, the sound of children's voices filled my ears, and I could see children singing whilst someone played the piano. It was quite enchanting. Of course, the group could not hear the music. When I described it to them, the owner of the brooch told me that her aunt used to take groups of children all over England to compete in choral competitions. She had been their music teacher.

I held the brooch for about another five minutes, but I only received information about the aunt, and nothing about the new owner.

She was disappointed, but I had to explain that the aunt's mind and those of the children, *en masse*, were more powerful than her own, and that these energies were blocking hers.

That is why it is best to give an object that has only been owned by you if you want some information about yourself.

The study of energy is extremely exciting. Matter is still energy, but it is a very dense type of energy.

Psychometry can provide you with a mass of information that would probably never otherwise be divulged. It has enabled me to help people by linking into vibrations they never realized were there.

One patient of mine failed to respond to healing. Although I used hypnotherapy, it was impossible to break down the barrier I knew was there, preventing her cure.

As she was leaving one day, I happened to pick up her spectacle case and was immediately given pictures of her being tormented by her husband. The vibrations I received were quite violent.

After asking her to sit down again, I described what I had seen. She broke down, sobbing, and told me everything. We talked about the problem for a while, and she left.

After this episode she responded to healing; she left her husband a year later.

Although I had asked many times about her home life, because I felt that she had a serious family problem, she had never mentioned the hurt she suffered. It had become an integral part of her life, and she accepted it as normal.

She had also depressed her mind energy so much that I did not receive it, either in my capacity as a medium or through hypnotherapy. But the energies had been absorbed by the spectacle case.

Psychometry is sometimes viewed as a game by those who know very little about it. It is far more than that, as you can see from the story above.

I believe it could be a tremendous aid in diagnosis – to find out what is really going on in the lives of sick people.

I must admit, though, that I have also had great fun using my psychometry skills, especially with a group of friends. One evening, sharing a glass of wine with a few friends, I asked one of the men for his ring. I described a few details of his life that I could 'see', then I received a picture of masses of women's underwear – mostly black. I pulled his leg, and asked him where he had been. He looked uncomfortable and blushed. His wife by this time was curious and not a little worried. She didn't own any black underwear. He left the room and came back with a package. 'If you must know,' he said. 'I was in a lingerie shop, buying Sheila a birthday present.' He opened the package. There were two pairs of black panties, a bra and a black see-through negligee. His wife stared at him, amazed. 'I never wear black,' she said. 'I know, but I thought if I was paying for them, I'd please myself as well!' he replied.

The pictures I had received were only a few hours old. One of the party was convinced that I had read the poor man's mind, and that I had not been using psychometry at all.

In fact, the feeling I have when receiving telepathy is entirely different to that when using psychometry. It is a more direct and clearer communication.

To prove to this person that it is possible to extract information from any object, I asked him to give me something belonging only to himself and that no-one else had handled. This he did.

I held the wallet that he had handed to me, felt the texture of the leather, and closed my eyes. I wanted to extract a memory he had forgotten so that telepathy could be ruled out.

It came. I asked him to accompany me to another room – amidst roars of laughter from the rest of the company.

I told him that it was an old memory that he had probably forgotten. It went back ten years. I could see him clearly in the pictures I was receiving, right down to the clothes he was wearing. I saw him turning his back on another person I knew to be a friend. 'You refused to help your best friend when he was in trouble,' I said, and he looked at me blankly. 'It was about ten years ago,' I went on. Shaking his head, he said, 'I'm sorry, I don't know what you are talking about. I would never turn my back on a friend.' 'Well, you did this time.' I placed my hand on his shoulder. 'And the reason was that he had stolen your girlfriend.' He stared at me in disbelief. 'My God! You're absolutely right,' he said 'I had completely forgotten. And it was that particular girlfriend that bought the wallet. I liked her very much at the time. My friend got into

financial difficulties over her, and I refused to help him.'
He could not believe that all this had been extracted from
an old wallet.

I have been asked many times to hold an object
hundreds of years old and describe where it came from.
These have been fascinating experiments, and I remember
one piece in particular.

It was handed to me in a parcel. I had no idea at the time
what it was. I closed my eyes – this helps as it shuts out
any other visual images – and after about five minutes gave
detailed information about the country and the original
owner of what I sensed to be a bracelet.

It came from Mexico, and had belonged to an Aztec
woman in the fourteenth century. I described valleys and
beautiful views. The pictures flowed one after another.
This person had lived in a type of commune and I could
see small groups of people sitting around a fire. I could see
the smoke very clearly. Suddenly, I felt quite woozy and I
was given the information that the owner of the bracelet
had died in childbirth.

The person who handed me the parcel told me that she
had no idea what was in it as it had been given to her by
someone who was actually sitting in another room. When
the owner entered the room later, he verified that it was
indeed an Aztec bracelet from the fourteenth century.

It is quite extraordinary how objects affect the manner-
isms of people, especially women who have been left
jewellery of some kind.

One lady I knew changed completely when she wore a
particular brooch. Her facial expressions changed, as did
the way she used her hands, the way she spoke and even
her walk. She just wasn't herself.

One day when we were having tea together, I asked her
who the brooch had belonged to. It was obvious that it was

quite old. She told me that it belonged to her great-grandmother, and showed me a sepia photograph. 'That was taken when she was quite young. I believe she was quite a strong character.' She laughed. 'She must have been – she had thirteen children.' The photograph was the exact likeness of this lady when she wore the brooch.

'Do you realize that your great-grandmother takes over when you wear that brooch?' And I described in detail how she changed.

She stared at me for a while, and I thought I had offended her. Then she said, 'You have confirmed something that I have felt every time I have worn it; I do *feel* different. But why?'

'It is quite obvious that your great-grandmother was a powerful person, because she has left the impression of her personality in the brooch.' I smiled at the look of disbelief on her face. I continued, 'When you wear it you are overshadowed by her.'

'Does that mean that I have a weak mind?' She looked slightly put out.

'No, not at all. It is just that she was a force to be reckoned with. There is nothing to worry about.'

'I must confess,' she said, 'that this has cleared up the feelings I have when I wear it. Do you think I should leave it in its case at home? It seems such a pity. It really is very beautiful.'

I assured her that there was no need to stop wearing it, but concluded that I thought she should wear it when she was being opposed. The character in the brooch would certainly be a tremendous asset under such circumstances.

It is also possible to deliberately impregnate an object, especially if this is for healing purposes.

At one time I kept a supply of handkerchiefs in my healing room so that they could absorb the energies, and used to send these out to sick people who were unable to visit me. I received some very interesting letters as a consequence.

I had sent one to a man who had terminal cancer of the stomach. He was receiving such large doses of morphine that he was usually unable to speak. From the time he received the handkerchief and placed it over his stomach, the doctor was able to reduce the dose considerably. His wife wrote to me: 'My husband and I cannot thank you enough for what you have done. He is able to hold conversations with me and his friends, and the pain is now bearable. Not only that, but when he closes his eyes he can see a woman sitting at a couch. I think it must be you.'

This was before I had written any books, and I sent them a photograph. Her husband confirmed that it was me that he could see. This surprised me because at that time I had believed that the handkerchiefs were only absorbing healing energy. Obviously, this was not so: my personality had also left its mark.

The energy I receive from paintings is quite extraordinary. I have only to look at a painting, or a print, to feel the mind waves of the artist.

These waves do not belong to the owner of the painting, but are inextricably bonded with the oils or watercolours. Oils in particular seem to capture and hold the mind waves.

Sometimes I have looked at a painting and have seen an energy picture superimposed on the original, which could be a room, a person or an energy pattern.

There is no doubt that the artist leaves a lifetime impression behind on the canvas. Perhaps this is why some people become obsessed with particular artists. They are drawn to the personality as well as the works.

Michelangelo's frescoes in the Sistine Chapel at Rome attract tourists and admirers from all over the world. When one considers the dedication and years spent on them, it is not surprising that they attract this sort of admiration. The talent and power of his mind waves encapsulated in the oils over such a long period must make a tremendous impression on all who see them.

I have always loved Claude Monet's paintings, especially 'Woman with a Parasol', which has a mystical quality to it, and was fortunate enough to be able to visit his home in Giverny, France.

I loved the famous green bridge that spanned the lake, with its equally famous waterlilies. The paintings were also inspiring – but the picture I carried away with me was not any of these things. It was the unbelievable sunflower yellow kitchen.

I have never entered a room that has had such an impact on me, and there was no doubt that Monet's soul was an integral part of it – due, no doubt, to the colour that he loved the most and the time he must have spent there.

Photographs are ideal for beginners, especially if they are of people. One can describe the personalities simply by holding the photograph.

By using this method, I have been able to give accurate information to the police about a murderer or a missing person.

Health problems can also be diagnosed and acted upon, especially when I give absent healing.

One lovely story is about two dachshunds called Misty and Mandy. The following is an excerpt from a letter written by their mistress.

Our little three-year-old dachshund, Misty, was diagnosed by our vet as having six calcified discs – three in the neck and three in the lower back. She was of course in considerable pain and this was kept under control with cortisone.

Purely by chance, my husband and I saw Betty Shine on a latenight television programme. We were very impressed by what we heard, and after much discussion, and a lot of scepticism, we agreed we had nothing to lose by writing to her for help with our little dog.

Betty replied and told us that all would be well! She was right; Misty progressed slowly and surely.

Unfortunately, three months later I had to write to Betty again, to inform her that lightning had struck in the same place twice. Our other dachshund, Mandy, who was then nine years old, had suffered the same fate. The X-rays showed that she had two calcified discs in her back. She was in great pain.

Again, Betty replied assuring me the dogs would be healed. She was correct. There was no instant cure, but they were progressing every day and within two months both dogs had fully recovered. I can honestly say that having seen the X-rays and witnessed the awful pain they both suffered – especially the younger one – it is nothing short of miraculous to see them romping and wrestling together, and living life to the full.

I was sent photographs of Misty and Mandy and worked with them all the time, linking into their energy counterparts so that I could stimulate their own self-healing abilities to decalcify the discs. It worked.

It should give writers great satisfaction to know that their energies are in every word they write.

No matter how many reprints there are of a book, the impression will still remain in the energy counterpart of that book. And no matter what the storyline, it will be the author's personality that will be picked up by anyone handling the book.

I have often picked up a book in a shop only to return

it instantly to the shelf. I could not open it and read it because of the vibrations. Interestingly, some of these books were supposed to be spiritual or religious.

I have often looked at titles of books in newspapers and known immediately which books are going to create trouble for the authors and the publishers.

On the other hand, there are books that have a wonderful healing quality about them and, once started, they are very difficult to put down. I have many such books in my own library.

I found that I could use psychometry on buildings by accident.

Whilst enjoying a lunch in an old country pub near Brighton many years ago, I happened to place my hand against the wall. I immediately received pictures of very nasty looking individuals – they were very scruffy and looked like pirates, with long boots and strange hats. There was a tremendous amount of activity in the scenes, then the scene shifted suddenly and I could see a man hanging from a large hook. I took my hand off the wall as I was beginning to feel slightly unwell. I didn't want to finish my lunch.

As we were leaving, my companion urged me to ask the proprietor if he knew the history of the place. He did. I then gave him a detailed description of what I had picked up and he laughed. 'You are absolutely right. They *were* pirates. There are numerous old tunnels leading from this place to the beach.' Then he smiled and asked me to look up. Immediately above my head was the hook. 'It has been there for hundreds of years. No-one has ever thought about removing it. I suppose it is proof that men were hung here.'

We listened for an hour whilst he told us all the gory

stories about the building. It had been a place of alcoholic refreshment even in those days.

The hate and fear that had evidently been in the ethos at the time of the hanging had blocked out all weaker vibrations, and that is why I had received such powerful impressions.

While at another inn, I decided to experiment again. The inn itself did not look as though it was very old, but it had an old coach house.

I placed my hand on the wall, and immediately received pictures of a very old building – structurally quite different from the modern pub in which we were sitting. I thought perhaps that the vibrations were incorrect. The scenes shifted all the time. The first was of a rather small room, with benches and tables. I couldn't see any people at first. Then I was in a larger room full of people dressed in very old-fashioned clothes. The men were wearing frilly cuffs and collars and the women wore cloaks.

Then I could see outside. There were horses and carriages and I could hear the noise of the horses' hooves. The yard was cobbled, and there were stables at the end of it.

I decided to speak to the owner. I told him what I had been doing, and described the scenes I had received. 'It didn't look anything like the present building,' I said.

'Well, you are absolutely correct,' he told me. 'At least about the structure of the old building, because I have the original plans that date back to 1750. It was eventually pulled down, and this place was built on the old site. The coach house is the original.' We followed him through a back door and there was the yard, exactly as I had seen it except, of course, there were no horses.

I found it quite extraordinary that the energies absorbed by the old building had been transferred to the new one.

The energies are obviously in a time capsule, and will penetrate any building that replaces the old one.

People very often become upset when a favourite hotel or restaurant is partly demolished so that the owners can extend the property. They believe the atmosphere will never be the same. But if it is an old place, it is quite possible that the vibrations will be held in a time capsule and, with a new addition, would be transferred to the whole – as in the previous story.

Churches are renowned for being peaceful. This is because they are places of worship, and usually the thoughts are spiritual. But I have known churches which have very unpleasant vibrations and, on studying the history, have found some unsavoury facts about the people who have 'prayed' in them.

If one walks into a building where several businesses have their offices, it is possible, by walking through the main door of each individual firm, to ascertain whether the employees are happy or not, or indeed whether you would like to work in any of them.

Everything absorbs information. If you want to learn how to extract secrets from inanimate objects, why don't you practise the following exercise.

Extracting Secrets

1 Ask a friend to give you something belonging to someone unknown to you. This is important because information and pictures can be clouded by the subconscious. The owner's permission must be given before the article is used for this purpose.

2 Sit down in a comfortable chair in a quiet room. Cup the object in your hands, and close your eyes. Now relax,

as though you are going to day-dream. Allow your mind to drift away from the object. *Do not even think about it.*

3 You will begin to feel sensations within your body. When this happens, link them up with *your* normal sensations. For instance, your stomach might start to rumble when you are frightened or when you have too much acidity. Perhaps you get pains in your stomach when you are emotionally upset. If you have these symptoms whilst holding the object and you did not have them immediately before you did so, then you are picking up the owner's problems. Always relate the feelings to your own, because you are interpreting them through your own energy counterpart. Sometimes you will find that your head aches. If you do not normally suffer with headaches, then again, the owner probably does.

It might be that you simply tune into that person's personality. Consequently, you will receive the good with the bad. Whatever you do, do not judge. That is not the purpose of the exercise.

When you feel that you have absorbed as much information as possible in a time limit of ten minutes, open your eyes and relax. Whatever you do, do not continue beyond that time as it will tire you.

4 If you have a photograph, follow the same procedure, studying it occasionally. Remember the most prominent features – these are usually the eyes, and the eyes are the mirror of the soul.

When you think you have a clear picture, close your eyes again and just think about it. It can be quite amazing when the information starts to flow. Sometimes it is like ticker-tape, moving so fast that it is difficult to remember it all.

Sometimes you will receive symbolism. For instance, if you have an impression of a fast flowing river, then it is probable that the owner's life is getting out of control. It could be that you will receive pictures or impressions of a cross. Be careful with this one – it may not necessarily mean that the person is religious. It might be that they may feel like a martyr.

A very common impression is of a bowl. Again this can be a tricky one. It could mean that the person will receive a gift – or that their life is like an empty bowl. It could even mean that the person is asking for help.

I have always found symbols confusing. It is much better to wait until you have very positive information and pictures. You will be on safer ground.

Whatever you do, do not make it up. You could find yourself in trouble and then your reputation will be shattered.

Enjoy your new hobby, knowing that it is increasing your sensitivity and awareness so that you will feel closer to others. The world would be in a worse state than it is at the moment without the sensitives who give love, sympathy and hope. Become one of these people. The world needs you.

PART FOUR

SENSES

16

Music to my Ears

My whole life has been linked with musicians and music.

My father's family were all artists: painters, singers and musicians, they were a very talented family.

From an early age we listened and sang to music, and I was hooked on singing from the age of two. There was always someone playing the piano, and I could not imagine a home without one.

Music has a dramatic effect on the mind. Each tone vibration is different, and consequently touches the different levels of mind energy.

I have noticed the effect that really beautiful music has on people. Their mind waves vibrate, and flow back and forth in harmony. That is why one can see that rapt look on their faces, as though they have shut the whole world out. In fact, they have. The waves lift and transport you into a realm that is dreamlike, taking pressure off the brain and body. Music is an essential part of any healing programme, and musicians all over the world have been experimenting with tones to soothe and heal the troubled mind and body.

Mantras have been used in Eastern religions for centuries, not only to soothe, but to reach a higher spiritual level. As a Wheel of Yoga teacher for twelve years, my daughter Janet used mantras in her classes, and the resulting relaxation, healing and spiritual levels that were attained were well worth all the effort she put into her teaching. She has also been recording mantras for many years, and these recordings have brought immense joy to hundreds of our clients all over the world. The letters we receive speak of the beauty of Janet's voice. She loves the mantras, and puts a lot of thought – and love – into every note, and her healing thoughts are a part of the whole. This is the secret of any successful performance.

Singers and musicians spend a lifetime learning their art, trying to achieve perfection; although that is a very rare commodity, they never stop trying. It is in their blood, their soul – which is the mind. The unity of the mind with like minds is the creator of genius. How is this achieved?

The first steps are extremely difficult, as in all things, and the noises produced can be painful to the ears. Many parents cannot stand the strain, and are relieved when their children give up trying. For those who have real talent, it is the love of the art that urges them on to greater heights. It is not always the children with most talent who are successful. Indeed, many children who have little talent to begin with but who love their music become the achievers. Tears are part and parcel of the learning process. Trying too hard can bring one down to rock bottom, and crying is a way of releasing tension. Also, amateurs learn that no matter how hard it may seem, they have to pick themselves up and start again. There is no easy way to the top in music; it is a gruelling road. Even the most ambitious can fall by the wayside if the love of music is not there. Why is this?

It is because the ambition for recognition is not enough. This is a selfish attitude, and therefore the mind energy does not expand enough to link in with minds of the truly powerful singers, musicians and composers of the past – a part of the Universal Mind, which contains all knowledge. Dedication to one's art has to be triggered by the *love* of one's art.

Many singers and musicians can feel the essence of a certain person linking with them when they are performing, and know instinctively what is expected of them. They have probably managed to have a mind-to-mind link with a composer at some time, and have thus absorbed part of their personality.

Great artists are those who are in love with their art, and this love affair lasts for the rest of their life. For them, there is no life without music, and music is energy.

A night at the opera, musical or concert can be a very powerful experience when there are great artists performing. It is a powerhouse of energy, where mind links with mind and everyone is in tune with each other. Whatever the artist gives out they receive back tenfold and more. The audience is with them all the way. This could not happen if mind waves did not exist, if all we had was our brain. Yes, we do have brain waves, inspiration, but only because the mind is pushing all the buttons.

I have watched the effect music has on mentally disabled children. They smile and hum, and rock themselves back and forth with joy. They do not understand the music itself, but they do understand vibrations, because they live on a vibrational level all the time. Although many of these children cannot make themselves understood to others, they are none the less able to appreciate what is going on around them. And they are able to feel at one with the waves of reverberating energy. It affects their whole being; they are inside something for once, instead of sitting on the outside. It represents a freedom they have never known, and they should never be without music in their lives.

I can remember, when I was a singer, the excitement of performing something I had spent months preparing. There is nothing quite like the feeling of adrenalin racing around the body, the lightness of the body as the mind expands, and that glorious feeling of lift-off – the first bars of music touching the soul, and the sensational feeling whilst singing of being in touch with something magical. It is sometimes very difficult to come back down to earth when this happens.

Maria Callas was at the height of her career when I was pursuing my own career – and this made me feel like giving up before I began. She was a magnificent actress, with a glorious voice. I am sure we will never hear the like of her again. I know there are wonderful women singers all over the world, but none have touched my soul the way Callas did.

She drew from a vast reserve of emotions, and used them skilfully in her dramatic singing and acting. She was a woman of the earth, with earthy passions that made people either love her or hate her, but no-one could ignore her. She was totally in love with her art. There is that word again – love. It gave Callas power, and she never wasted it. It was the power of her mind that enabled her to sing and act as she did, and like anyone in tune with themselves and their soul, she touched other souls.

The same can be said for the superb Pavarotti. I remember looking at a televised programme from Italy when he and his father were singing in their local church, and the joy on their faces as they sang together was a sight to behold. That joy was carried around the world for all to see and feel. They had love for each other, and for their music, and this showed in their performance.

Pavarotti is unique. The power of the mind and total love for the music creates the same unbeatable combination.

Love in its purest form is the most powerful energy in the Universe.

Popular singers who touched my soul were Nat King Cole, and Frank Sinatra in his heyday. They had the magical combination of being able to manipulate the emotions and wring every drop of blood out of the words.

Everyone, musical or otherwise, can have the same feelings by simply listening to a beautiful piece of music of their choice. Why not try the following exercise so that you can touch the soul of the composer and/or performer. If you do not live alone, listen to the music in your bedroom.

Touching the Soul

1 Tune into the music of your choice. Sit on the floor with your arms around your knees. Close your eyes.

2 As you listen, rock back and forth very gently, in time with the rhythm.

3 Become aware of the vibrations within your body and allow the tensions to ease away.

4 When you feel that you are a part of the performance change position. Sit crosslegged, with the palms of your hands on your knees, eyes closed.

5 At this point you should feel light and heady. Allow yourself the freedom of being in a timeless situation. Stay in this position until the performance is finished, and give yourself a further three minutes to return to normal.

Because you have something specific to think about during

the performance, your mind will not wander, and this enables you to channel your thoughts.

Disciplining your Thoughts

Disciplining and channelling your thoughts can also be of immense benefit in other areas of your life. This exercise has been devised to help you in this way.

1　Choose a quiet place, sit down and relax. Breathe deeply three times. Close your eyes.

2　Think of a nursery rhyme, and visualize each word as though it was alive. Now repeat the verse in your mind and, as you do so, follow the words as they walk down a corridor. Think of them as children. If you see one of them disappearing into a door off the corridor, guide it back to the mainstream. *Remember you are always in control.*

3　When they have reached the end of the corridor – it does not matter how long it takes – bring them back again. Because the words have a mind of their own, the journey back could be very frustrating, so keep your eyes on every word-child and do not allow your mind to stray.

If you have been evolving through the exercises in *Mind Magic* you should find this exercise very easy. If you find it difficult just *know* that the words are walking down the corridor. Knowing is just as powerful as visualizing.

This kind of discipline is needed in all voice training.

I love listening to beautiful speaking voices. They are indeed music to my ears. The most beautiful male voice I have ever heard was that of Richard Burton, the actor.

What a pity that he did not do more theatre in his later years. I believe the timbre of the voice is lost in films – it is the sound reverberating around the theatre that touches the soul. If God has a voice I am sure it would sound like his. His Welsh background must have had a lot to do with it. I believe that listening to the singing voices of the valleys from birth must have left a permanent imprint on his mind; he enchanted me with the end product.

It is also a pity that schools do not give any time at all to voice production or to elocution. There is no point in gaining 'A's in English if you are unable to articulate correctly.

Through my mediumship, I have been shown concerts in other dimensions. Whilst in this energy state I heard music in an entirely different way: there were shafts of colour changing with every tone, and it seemed as though the colour itself was indeed the music. It sounded as though I was in a vast hall, with a hundred echoes. Perhaps this vast hall was the Universe. These moments have been rare and have left an indelible mark on my mind.

My favourite instruments are the violin, clarinet, flute, piano and trumpet, all beautifully played of course. There are so many wonderful musicians in the world and they all bring a healing quality into our lives. I would like to name Yehudi Menuhin as the finest musical healer. It is not only his fine musicianship that is so incredible, but also the man himself. Having studied and practised yoga all his life, he emanates a spirituality and peace that no other musician – in my opinion – has been able to emulate. By example, he teaches the power of peace. This is an extraordinary gift and when linked to his great talent, what else can one ask for? The vibrations of his playing lift the listener into a different dimension so that one has a feeling of weightlessness, and every sound is similar to those in my other-dimension concerts. One finds that same feeling of peace, without the musical talent, in the presence of great spiritual teachers.

The only spiritual teachers I have known, are, indeed, in spirit. But I have heard from many people that the peace experienced in the presence of great gurus is exactly the same.

They do not have to work at being spiritual – they are *of* spirit. That is to say they are able to move about in different dimensions with no effort at all, and therefore stress has no meaning for them. To be in the company of someone who is not giving out stress vibrations is a rare experience, and one that we should all try to imitate.

Try the following anti-stress exercise.

Relieving Stress

1   Choose a nice, quiet room, preferably carpeted. Now lie down on the floor and close your eyes.

2   Breathe deeply three times. Try to breathe through your nose so that the air makes a slight hissing sound as you breathe in. Hold the third breath for as long as possible, then let it out in small puffs. As you do this, you will feel energy circulating throughout your body and you will begin to feel warm. You may also feel a bit light-headed, if so, do not hold your breath for so long next time. Repeat three times.

3   Now visualize energy building up underneath your body, little by little, until it is a solid mass. When you are successful with this part of the exercise, move on.

4 You will feel at this point as though you are going to levitate, and that you are in a dream-state. Forget everything and enjoy every minute. Stay with it.

5 When you are ready, visualize the energy gradually disappearing, and feel your body getting heavier and heavier. Open your eyes.

6 Give yourself about five minutes before attempting to get up. When you do, move very gently.

What happened during this exercise to take the stress out of your mind and body? I will tell you. The whole of your energy-counterpart and mind energy were released, taking the pressure off your physical body and allowing it to breathe, to vibrate, and the life-force to circulate. That is why you felt warm at one point. Or perhaps you felt a nice warm feeling all the time. If so, so much the better. It really does not matter, but it does give you an indication of how much pressure you are releasing.

Another way of relieving stress is to listen to our song-birds. There is no finer music to my ears. The nightingale, thrush, mistle-thrush, blackbird, robin, linnet, finch, nut-hatch, tits – there are so many.

I remember one magical day when a charm of gold-finches danced and twittered at the end of my garden, feeding on the thistles and groundsel. They looked like a moving cloth of gold, a rare and precious moment in time.

The nightingales in France late at night are another beautiful memory. The flute-like sound remains with me always. The song thrush certainly lives up to its repu-tation, singing for many minutes at a time. The mistle-thrush has shorter, flutier, notes, and is known as the storm cock because it sings on throughout the cold wintry days. The blackbirds are always there singing their hearts out. What a joy they are, delivering their song from the treetops, their warbling punctuated by pauses as they breathe like prima donnas.

Whilst walking around the garden one day I heard the most enchanting warbling. It was quite beautiful, but I could not place the bird and I thought it must be some rare species. Imagine my surprise when I eventually tracked it down to a robin. I had no idea that robins had such a beautiful song.

The only caged bird I have ever owned was a linnet-canary cross. Its song filled the house. It had a room to itself, with perches under a fanlight covered with mesh. My daughter used to play her guitar in that room, and the linnet sang louder and louder as she played, trying to compete. The linnet always won. Although it had so much freedom, I grieved about its confinement, but felt that I could not free it as it would probably die. After three years it managed to free itself, and I was relieved, but our home was never the same without its incredible song. Fortunately, I taped its performances. Unfortunately wild linnets are rare nowadays because of the increasing use of weed-killers which has depleted their food supply. But when one is lucky enough to hear them, it is food for the soul.

The chaffinch is another bird that has been affected by toxins and the disappearance of the hedgerows. Now that farmers are actually replanting hedgerows, perhaps their numbers will increase, and we will see the unmistakable colours more frequently in our gardens as well as hearing their distinctive song – which varies from region to region.

The common blue tit is loved by everyone until it steals the cream off the milk. With its blue head, yellow under-parts and familiar trill it would be difficult to imagine a country garden without them. I also love the plaintive call of the coal-tit, white beneath a black cap, and the crested tit, with its distinctive rattling trill which one can hear in pine forest or woodland. The warbling of the willow tit and the scolding sound of the marsh tit add to this delightful group.

Birds, like ourselves, are dependent on water which is another special sound. I love the sound of waterfalls, falling from a great height. On a hot sunny day the sound of the rushing water is reminiscent of the sounds I have when moving from one dimension to another. Our garden waterfalls cannot match these dramatic displays, but they are certainly better than none at all. A trout stream, with its flashes of silver as the fish move swiftly beneath the sparkling water, and the trickling tinkling sound as it passes over the large round stones is a joy to my ears.

And as for the sea, well, what can one say that has not already been said a hundred times. The vast, varying oceans of water are a completely different world to that of land, and yet both exist on the one planet. The sound of the sea crashing against the rocks on a stormy day is dramatic in its intensity. The sound of waves breaking on the shore, and the sound of the sand and stones being dragged out to sea as it retreats, are music to my ears. Lying on the beach with eyes closed, one can for a few fleeting moments disappear into a timeless dimension, whilst people splash about, screaming and laughing in the waves.

Laughter is perhaps the most important sound of all, because it doesn't need any special setting. We can laugh wherever we are, and laughter creates vibrations which are at the very centre of healing.

In this chapter I have given you all the things that are Music to my Ears, and described how the vibrations lift the energies, and take the pressure off our mind and body.

The mind waves created by these vibrations have an unbelievable effect on everything around us, and they continue to extend outwards beyond our physical beings. They reach out and link up with cosmic force, which in turn is relayed back to us tenfold. We are in fact sending out messages of love, hope and beauty. That is why I was so interested in an extract from *Science News* that was sent to me by a client.

January 1988 (AP) Bored with tedious mathematical equations, a Japanese geneticist, Susumu Ohno, decided to convert the genetic patterns of living cells into musical notation. He thought that listening to genetic codes, rather than staring at them, would make patterns easier to detect. In this process he discovered that genes not only carry the blueprint of life, they also carry a tune.

Translated into sheet music, a portion of mouse ribonucleic acid sounds like a lively waltz, very similar to Chopin's Nocturne, Opus 55, No. 1. The notes derived from the genetic codes are NOT just random notes that some geneticists predicted, but genuine music of the Baroque and Romantic eras, with an uncanny similarity to the works of great composers.

Interestingly, the musical score derived from cancer cells sounds very sombre, while the musical coding of the gene that gives transparency to the eye is filled with trills and flourishes, and is airy and light. Mr Ohno said, 'What I think is at work here are underlying principles that govern the structure of many things – a gene, a birdsong, a musical composition.'

I find this very interesting, because when I am giving trance healing I am very often listening to 'out of this world' music.

Vibrations are at the root of life, and vibrations form themselves into patterns which in turn create sound which is musical. Nature left alone would never be the creator of something that was unmusical; everything in Creation is harmonious – it is only man who has tried to spoil it all.

I have listed all the things that are Music to my Ears. Why not make your own list? It is only by doing so that you will recognize all the wonderful sounds that have affected your own mind waves, and that you have previously taken for granted. And the majority of them are free.

17

The Colours of my Life

Colour has always played an important part in my life. As a child the way I felt depended entirely on what colour I was wearing. I loved blue – it always gave me peace.

One of my first memories was of the knitted garments my mother and aunt used to make, and the balls of wool that were made from skeins hanging on the back of a chair. Or, more often, over my hands. I was so fascinated that I rarely noticed my aching arms until the job was finished.

Another early memory is of my most treasured possession: a kaleidoscope, which, when turned, changed into beautiful patterns and a profusion of bright colours. I spent hours gazing through the tube and wondering how it worked its magic.

I was also aware of colours that did not exist in this dimension, as I have mentioned in my previous books. This perception may have given me a greater insight into colour. For instance, I knew that colours were made up of particles of different shades, and that the majority determines the first impression. Nothing in this world or others is as it seems. It is being able to see the hidden depths that brings a magic into our lives.

I remember the beautiful day lilies my mother grew in our small garden in London. There was no grass in the garden, just a small patch of concrete with a flower border. This was empty, most of the time, except for the lilies.

They were creamy white, tinged with pink and with orange stamens, and to me, they symbolized a beauty rarely seen in the area in which I lived. I longed to see more flowers in that small garden. My love of flowers started with those lilies, and now I am never happy unless I have borders or containers of brightly coloured flowers in the garden and a profusion of cut flowers in my home.

There is something so wonderful about nature. From perfectly ordinary bulbs come an array of leaves and multicoloured flowers that never cease to amaze me. From a few dried roots comes a fantastic display in the herbaceous border that delights the eye all summer. Prickly bushes, trees, climbers and ramblers all bearing the most exquisite roses; where else can one feel the texture and bouquet of the deep red velvet rose? Nor must I forget the wild flowers that give an endless display all year: the magnificent carpets of bluebells, primroses and aconites that we chance upon in our woods. And the disappearing beauty of the woodland foxgloves. They all bring an endless variety of colour in this sometimes grey world. In the summer, bright red poppies covering the countryside bring gladness into our lives. With colour all is not lost, there is hope.

Shrubs give us a variety of flowers all year: winter-flowering cherry, heather, forsythia – that magical shrub that brightens up the most boring patches in the garden on cold wintry days; the amazing variety of rhododendrons and azaleas, lilac, and the wonderful buddleia that attracts the most colourful butterflies. The list is endless, but most people, at some time or another, have had these ordinary shrubs in their gardens and have been affected by them. That is why these plants are so marvellous. Whether you notice them or not, they still flower and attract rays that are beneficial to all nature and to ourselves. Knowing about energy opens up a beautiful new landscape that you have never experienced before. Think about it.

I must not forget the exquisite bouquets of flowers that are seen in the florists' shop throughout the year: daffodils, tulips, carnations, roses, daisies, scabious, lilies and chrysanthemums with their beautiful shades of autumn.

Trees are there for everyone to enjoy even at great distances and the following pages list my favourites. There are those wonderful majestic oaks, the English oaks. Druids gathered mistletoe from the oak boughs for their sacred rites in Celtic England, and as a child, I thought the acorns and their cups were pure magic. Conditions in an oak forest support other trees such as the hazel, holly and ash because the oak tree has a wonderful open canopy. It sustains everything beneath it. The quickly rotting oak leaves provide cover for many insects and animal life, and the leaves themselves make the best leaf mould. The colours of the oaks, from bright green to darker hues to the exquisite colours of autumn are there for all to appreciate.

The scarlet oak provides some of Britain's most stunning autumn colours, and is seen in parks and along roadsides – mainly because it cannot tolerate shade. Red oaks are planted for autumn colour, as their leaves turn a beautiful dark red at that time of year.

The list of oaks is numerous, and our countryside is the richer for their presence.

The beech, a tracery of bright green in the spring as the leaf buds burst, to an amazing display of autumn colours that range from yellow and orange through to red-brown and the deeper tones of the copper beech. The beech nuts are highly prized by wood mice and squirrels, and the density of the canopy during the summer keeps the ground dry and comfortable for woodland creatures. Bluebells and wood anemones survive and grow beneath the beech trees before the canopy of leaves has fully opened.

The horse chestnut has candles of flowers in the spring, which brighten up the roadsides and verges. In the autumn, when the soft green covering releases the conkers, schoolboys scour the ground for the prize specimen so that they can beat all-comers. The shiny brown of the new conkers gives a new dimension to parks and gardens.

The Indian horse chestnut blooms about seven weeks after the common horse chestnut, and is being used more frequently to extend the flowering season and delight the eye of the passer-by.

The hawthorn tree is another common tree that brightens up the countryside with its early flowers and late berries.

The rowan tree, or mountain ash as it is usually known, is lovely and graceful. It was often planted in churchyards to ward off witches. The sharp pointed leaves, which turn red in autumn, are a delight, as are the red berries which the birds feast on for their winter supply of vitamins. Bird catchers once used the berries to trap thrushes, redwings and other birds.

The elder is another hedgerow tree that flowers in spring and produces autumn berries, which hang in beautiful big bunches, easy pickings for the ardent fan of elderflower cordial, wine and jam. It is very rich in vitamin C.

All of the pines give pleasure, especially in forests, and are lovely to see in small groups where the landscape is otherwise desolate.

I have mentioned but few of our wonderful trees but those listed above are the most common, there for all of us to enjoy.

The sweeping fields of ripe corn, wheat and barley are glorious to behold, along with the beautiful yellow of rape and mustard.

Seascapes are a favourite of mine. The colours keep in tune with the sky – grey with white foam one minute, blue and white the next as the clouds roll by, giving us a glimpse of the sun.

In brighter climes, the silver fish seen beneath the surface bring a new dimension to this watery world, as do the delicate corals of pinks and white, and the shiny green fronds of seaweed moving with the motions of the tides.

When I lived in Spain my villa overlooked a valley which led to the sea. The sunsets viewed from the balcony were spectacular and I have always missed the beautiful red and orange, sometimes tinged with yellow as shafts of light came through the clouds. It was a beautiful sight.

The huge autumn moon was also a sight to behold. I would never have believed that the moon could look so huge. In certain climatic conditions it sometimes looked almost silver, but it was usually a deep, creamy yellow. I have never forgotten it, and the memories and pleasure those sightings gave me remain with me always.

The mountains of Spain were also a source of joy. I often visited an inland village that was perched on top of a mountain, reached by walking up a steep cobbled road or riding on a donkey. I preferred to walk, and it was worth every gasping breath when I finally reached the top and could look down on a turquoise lake, haunting, magical and peaceful.

The markets were an inspiration, with brightly coloured scarves, and rolls of silks imported from the east. Stalls were filled with ornate garments embroidered with bright silks by the local women. Pure white lace, beautiful in its neutrality, was lovely to see.

Vegetable markets were a delight to my eye, green peppers, oranges, apples of varying colours, the yellow of honeydew melons in huge piles, and the large green shape of the watermelon already cut in slices, deep red and white; the deep yellow and green of the bananas, red-orange of the carrots, the onions with their shiny outer skins, parsnips and purple-cream swedes, and so much more. There were tomatoes such as we have never seen in Britain – large, red and ripe. Everything glowed with the colours that only almost-permanent sunshine can achieve.

I missed the sun, the moon and the stars when I returned to England. I also missed the vibrant colours of Spain – but I know that we can brighten our lives wherever we are, by adding different hues to our surroundings, and in our wardrobe.

One has only to experience the gloom of a winter's day to know that without colour in our lives all the time, depression would be our permanent bedfellow. Colour attracts the cosmic rays, which enhance and stimulate our energy system. By merely thinking of a colour you will attract these rays.

Most of the time, people are not aware that they are being affected by colour. So common are the sights I have mentioned that they sometimes cease to have a physical impact, but colour always has an impact on the mind, and it is this that triggers off the familiar energy pattern of attraction. Without colour there would be no life.

I mentioned colour healing in *Mind Magic*. Use colour for healing; it is extremely powerful and brings wonderful results. Buy an array of coloured scarves to aid the healing process.

Now that you have read about the colours in my life, why not write down your own list. I think you would be surprised by the way in which colours have, perhaps unknowingly, affected your life.

Better still, bring even *more* colour into your life, and surround yourself with energy and beauty.

18

Birds

The great majority of us take birds for granted. They are always there, in the garden and in the countryside. Unfortunately, familiarity can mean that we do not care enough to study their habits.

Most people do not even realize that birds that were around in summer have disappeared in the winter. They are not concerned, and consequently do not know that the birds make hazardous journeys around the world, finding better climatic conditions where they breed. Then in the spring, they make the same journeys back to their original homes.

That they find their way there and back is amazing. What sort of map do they use? They can even return to a particular house – a quite extraordinary phenomenon. We take it for granted that they will return, but we give little thought to the obstacles that we create in their path.

Many of those who do not return, and they can be counted in thousands, die as a result of being caught in the fires of oil rigs which have been built in the migration path. I remember watching a programme on television where the birds were, quite literally, flying into the fire and dropping onto the rig and into the water, blackened and burned beyond recognition.

Why do they fly into the fire and not around it? I believe that over countless years, the different species have followed a network of energy lines, similar to the network I have created for absent healing. These energy lines can be miles apart but still follow the same direction. That is why birds spread themselves out and do not bump into each other. If some of the birds are following a specific line that carries them over the oil-rig fires, then they will try to fly through it. It is rather like embarking on a train journey. One cannot jump out of one train into another just because there is an obstruction ahead.

Scientists believe that birds follow the sun and various magnetic lines. They may be correct in their assumptions. After all, mind energy is magnetic.

But that still does not answer the question of how the birds return year after year, not only to the same area, but to the same house, making their nests in exactly the same spot for years. House martins are but one of the many species who carry out this unbelievable achievement.

I believe that their old nests act as radar stations and they follow the beam. They know exactly where they made their nests, and they have an accurate mind map which pinpoints the same area and building they used the previous year.

Migrating birds are a typical example of the use of mind waves. What else could possibly achieve the miracle of migration year after year? How can one dismiss the energy world when simple creatures can achieve so much by using this energy.

The whole universe is criss-crossed with networks of energy lines. Most of them haven't even been tapped yet.

First we have to accept that they are there. Then who knows what wonders we may achieve. Like so many things in this world, it is possible that by studying something as natural as bird migration we could find the key to this planet's energy network.

PART FIVE

ESOTERIC

19

The Guru

The cave was set deep in the mountains. There were carpets on the floor, and lighted candles shone from niches cut into the walls. The ceiling was curved, carved out of the solid rock, and its surface had a polished, ethereal look to it. A subtle fragrance pervaded the atmosphere.

In the centre of the cave, the guru sat motionless, his eyes closed, lost in meditation. His body was invisible beneath the folds of a white robe, and his long white hair fell about his shoulders, framing the golden complexion of his face. An aura of total peace and serenity surrounded him.

Suddenly, he opened his eyes and smiled. His dark brown eyes were lit from deep within by an unbelievable radiance.

'Please come in,' the guru asked, though no sound had come from the cave's entrance.

At once, people began to slip silently into the cave. They had come from far and wide, drawn by many different hopes and needs. Now they came together, sitting cross-legged on the carpets as they took their places in the gathering. The guru watched, and his smile touched them all.

'Welcome,' he said simply, then turned to a young girl who was sitting near to him. 'Tell me, what is your name and why have you come here?'

'My name is Pamela,' the girl replied. 'And I have come to listen and to learn.' She seemed reluctant to say any more and her eyes were downcast, but the guru knew of her real need.

'Pamela,' he said gently, 'something is troubling you. If you would like to share the problem with us, perhaps we can help you. We are a family here and the love that has united us will also ensure that everything that is said here today will be safeguarded and confidential. You may speak freely.' His voice was reassuring and Pamela hesitated only for a moment.

'I lost my mother a year ago. She was my life!' The words tumbled out in a rush, and she burst into tears.

'Let us all share her tears,' the guru responded, 'and feel her grief.' As he spoke, tears began to fall from his own eyes, and others also cried, silently. Minutes passed and gradually the tears ceased. Eventually, Pamela dried her eyes and smiled bravely.

'Thank you,' she whispered. 'That's the first time I've ever been able to release my emotions.'

'Why haven't you been able to cry before?' the guru asked.

'Where I come from,' she answered, 'people are embarrassed if you cry.'

'But you see around you people from all over the world who have shared your grief and are not embarrassed,' he exclaimed. He indicated the rest of the gathering and Pamela looked around at the tear-stained faces and felt their support and strength. 'When you go back home, seek out those who will do likewise,' the guru went on. 'Perhaps you need to think about your choice of companions.'

Then speaking once again to the whole group, he added, 'Let us now sit quietly and visualize the friends we would like for Pamela. Picture them reaching out and touching her, comforting her and listening to her words, enfolding her in their warm, unselfish love. Do not worry if you cannot visualize them clearly. Simply *know* that they are there – and they will be there.'

The guru paused and closed his eyes before speaking again.

'After that, let us surround Pamela with a golden glow of spirituality and peace.'

Minutes passed in complete silence as they all set their minds to the task. And then, suddenly, the entire cave was bathed in a golden light. The people who were watching gasped and the others opened their eyes immediately. It was a truly magical sight.

Around the guru's head was a brilliant, golden halo which expanded to shine even beyond the confines of the cave, reaching out and finding the Source. Everyone sat mesmerized until the halo retracted and the guru opened his eyes once more.

'And what is your name?' he asked a young man, speaking as though nothing out of the ordinary had occurred.

'My name is Sam.' The young man's eyes were still wide with wonder.

'You are very sad,' the guru said. 'How would you like me to help you?'

At this, Sam's face fell as he remembered his own concerns.

'I'm unhappy,' he replied wearily, 'because I was born ugly. Beauty means everything in this materialistic world.'

'That is a very sweeping statement,' the guru remarked. 'When you look in the mirror, does your image offend you so much? Isn't there anything you like about yourself?'

'I like my eyes,' Sam answered hesitantly.

'The eyes are the mirror of the soul,' the guru

explained. 'That is why you have beautiful eyes. An ordinary mirror cannot show the beauty of the soul and perhaps, for a time, you should not look into a mirror. People who have a purpose in life have very little time for such things. I do not even own a mirror. I would have no use for it.

'In this dimension, the casing which your soul inhabits is the only thing one can see,' he continued, 'unless your soul is advanced. The packaging can be ugly or beautiful but it is of no real significance in the end.'

'In my heart I know that,' Sam said. 'But how can I be happy in this dimension?'

'You must rearrange your thoughts,' the guru answered promptly. 'Let me give you an example. There have been many successful actors who were, and are, ugly. If you look at some of the great orators, their faces are alive, changing all the time. Their looks are of no importance. They are entertaining because they have a light which shines from within. You are impressed by their talent, not by their features – and a beautiful person who is a bad actor will never truly impress anyone.'

He paused to allow the truth of his words to sink in and then continued.

'There are people in all walks of life who are success-ful and ugly. They spend their lives working for their success and have very little time to worry about whether they are beautiful or not. They have a mission and their whole lives are directed towards accomplishing that mission. The whole world respects success and admires those who achieve it, regardless of what they look like on the surface.'

'Why don't you look deep into your heart to find your talent. Give it time to develop and seek your own measure of success. Working hard is a cure for many things, because there is not time to dwell on trivialities. Be true to your soul and you will be happy. Then, when you look in the mirror, you will see a person whose face is animated, whose expression changes all the time – a person with enthusiasm for life.'

'I will try,' Sam promised.

'One last thing,' the guru said smiling. 'Remember that beauty truly is in the eye of the beholder. If someone hates you, they will see you as ugly. But if you are loved, then you will be beautiful to the person that loves you. It's as simple as that.'

The guru shut his eyes and stretched out his arms. With his long, slim fingers spread, he looked as though he was blessing everyone. Silence descended throughout the cave until he abruptly opened his eyes again and said, 'I would like to speak to Miriam.'

'I am Miriam.' The voice came from a small figure at the back of the cave. She sounded not in the least surprised that the guru knew her name.

'You have a wonderful glow around you, Miriam,' he responded. 'Can you tell me what has entered your life since you have been here?'

'Knowledge,' she answered simply.

'Why should knowledge give you such light?'

Miriam thought for a moment before answering.

'When we are listening and absorbing knowledge,' she began, 'we relax and our minds are able to link up with cosmic forces. Our mind energy is strengthened and revitalized and so it expands beyond where we are – outside of this cave,' she added, gesturing at the stone walls. 'When we were helping Pamela, you were glowing when your mind energy returned.'

The guru's pleasure at her words was plain for all to see.

'Here we have a person who is not only spiritual and observant, but also psychic,' he said. 'Is that not so?'

'Yes. That is so,' Miriam admitted, sounding oddly reluctant and obviously aware that many of the others were looking at her.

'Why did you come here today?' the guru asked.

'As I become more spiritual,' she replied, 'I also feel an increasing responsibility towards others. You see . . . I often know what they are thinking . . . and frequently it disturbs me. I don't know how to handle it. There's no fun in my life at the moment.'

'You must always remember we are living in a physical world,' he told her calmly. 'In this dimension, we should enjoy our physical pleasures as well as the spiritual side. Life is for living, for giving – but also for receiving. Don't let your awareness blind you to that.'

'But those who are not aware bore me,' Miriam protested.

'That is not their fault,' the guru replied. 'Perhaps the time is not right for them to become aware. Perhaps you are shutting people out now that you are aware.'

'Perhaps,' she said thoughtfully.

'Have you ever thought that you may bore them with *your* presence?' he asked. 'They don't need lectures. Show them more love. After all, who wants to mix with a saint when all you want is to have fun?' He was smiling and his expression was mischievous. His dark eyes sparkled.

'I understand,' Miriam said, smiling back. 'I must strike a balance. Of course. It's so obvious now. I have been imbalanced. Thank you.'

'I have given you very little,' he responded. 'You have worked it out for yourself. The answers to our problems lie within us. Unlocking them is the real problem.' Then looking round at the gathering as if he was somehow

186

measuring them, he said, 'I would like you all to close your eyes and hold out your hands, palms upwards.'

There was silence while they obeyed. A minute later he asked, 'Can you feel your hands tingling?'

Several people answered, 'Yes.' Some murmured tentatively; others were more confident and firm. A few did not speak at all but nodded, forgetting that no-one could see them.

'Would you like to see the energy that is making your hands tingle?' the guru asked.

Again they answered in the affirmative.

'Then open your eyes.'

Gasps of surprise filled the cave as they obeyed him and stared at the spinning spirals of energy that whirled in the palms of their hands. The ever-shifting colours were extraordinarily beautiful.

The guru laughed at their amazement. 'In future,' he told them, 'you will know what is happening when your hands tingle.' He moved his hands and, as the others followed his example, the spirals vanished.

'Is it always like that, or does it only happen when you are present?' a man who had not spoken before asked.

'When you open your hands, palm upwards,' the guru replied, 'you are expecting to receive. It is an invitation. All is known to the Source. Consequently you will receive energy to revitalize you.'

'Can you tell us more about energy?' a young girl requested. 'For instance, is it possible that one day I will be able to *see* energy, like I did just now?' Her eyes were still wide with excitement.

'That rather depends on how you progress,' he answered and then, seeing her confusion, he went on. 'It is not a question of sitting for hours meditating or using similar exercises,' he told her kindly. 'It is a question of how you live your life. However spiritually advanced you appear to be, the soul knows the truth and so, if you are not truly spiritual, gifts will not be given to you.'

'What is the soul?' someone else asked.

'The mind has many levels and the soul is one of these,' the guru replied. 'At the soul level, it has infinite energy. Remember – all energy has different levels.'

'How do these levels work in conjunction with each other?' the questioner persisted, sounding uncertain.

'It is not as difficult as you might think,' the guru answered, smiling. 'Materialistic thoughts use the denser mind energy that is the nearest to the physical body. As your thoughts become less self-centred and unselfish, love enters your life, and the finer and less obvious parts of the mind energy are developed.

'The soul cannot be seen. As the most extreme part of your mind, it is always in contact with levels that are unknown to most people. Nevertheless, messages are passed through all the levels of the mind – from the soul to the most materialistic – to help and sustain us.'

'So, in a way, the soul tries to lift us,' Miriam added. 'But how can we know when this is happening?'

'Everything is known at soul level,' the guru responded. 'When you are trying to help yourself, certain truths will be made known to you. And then you begin your voyage of discovery. There will be many pitfalls along the way – and you will be helped only very occasionally.'

'That's right,' Miriam put in eagerly. 'Sometimes nothing seems worthwhile but then, from out of the blue, something happens to lighten your life – not materialistically, but something much more valuable – love, friendship, or being shown a different path. For instance, I am always guided to read the books that enhance my knowledge of life – not necessarily spiritual books, but those that encompass all life.'

'Yes,' the guru agreed enthusiastically. 'You will also find that this knowledge will bring with it certain spiritual gifts that will enable you occasionally to touch the soul level. One of these gifts is "knowing".'

'I have that gift,' Miriam said, 'but I have never been able to describe it properly.'

'Think of all the examples in your life,' he suggested. 'When somebody loves you, it is obvious without the need for words. You *know* they love you. Hate is equally obvious. If you have children, you *know* when there is something wrong, even if there are no obvious signs of a problem. It is a feeling within you.

'Outside of family and friends, the knowing may work in a slightly different way. For example, you can walk into a room and sense the atmosphere. Immediately, you *know* whether you want to stay or not.

'It can also work over long distances. You may suddenly *know* that someone is in trouble and then telephone or write to them to ask after their health. You would be pleasantly surprised at how often you were right. It really is a question of tuning into yourself and your higher mind or soul.'

'Is the higher mind the same as the soul?' a young man asked.

'No, but it is one of the higher levels, nearest the soul,' the guru replied, 'and it can be a great source of comfort because it is a powerful communicating bridge between the levels.'

'I think I know what you mean,' a lady called Natalie commented. 'Sometimes, after meditating or just day-dreaming, I am given the answers to problems.'

'As you progress, you will be given knowledge

automatically,' he responded, nodding, 'as though some-one had given you second sight. All of these levels are far more exciting than anything on the physical level.' With that, the guru ended that part of their discussion. 'Now I would like you to close your eyes again,' he instructed. 'Be still.'

As the minutes passed silently, everyone became aware of some kind of energy swirling around the cave.

'Are you tingling all over?' the guru asked eventually.

'Yes,' most of them replied, wondering what new marvels were to be shown to them.

'If any among you do not feel the energy,' the guru said, 'direct your thoughts towards me.' More time passed and the level of anticipation grew until he added. 'Now open your eyes and look at each other.'

Mouths dropped open and eyes went wide in astonish-ment as they looked at their neighbours. There, for all to see, were the seven chakras, swirling vortices of energy. They had all known of the chakras in theory, but none had actually seen them before. The spirals upon their palms had been entrancing, but this beautiful display made them all feel ecstatic.

On each person, the chakras were positioned at the top of the head, in the middle of the forehead – the third eye – at the throat, heart, spleen and navel and, at the base of the spine, the kundalini chakra, in all its splendour. All of them shone with different colours – even those in similar positions – and the guru explained that this was due to the differing levels of spirituality of each person there. All too soon, he asked them to shut their eyes again and, as they did so, the tingling left their bodies and was replaced by a feeling of peace.

'I want you all to meditate now,' the guru said, 'or if you

are not used to that, allow your mind to be free, to day-dream.'

The cave was suddenly filled with music, indescribably lovely and certainly not of this world, as minds reached hitherto unknown levels. A sense of oneness pervaded the whole cave. In that time it was impossible to differentiate between one body and another, and, for the first time, everyone there understood the oft-heard advice about the necessity of all parts becoming the whole. Now they were in a place where thought was no longer necessary and, indeed, impossible.

The guru's voice sounded again, as if from a void.

'You have all become part of each other. Now I am going to bring you back.' Seconds later he told them to open their eyes and sat smiling at them all. 'You have been blessed,' he said.

There was silence for a while as they all collected their thoughts, remembering the extraordinary events of the past few minutes.

'Something like that happened to me before,' a man named John ventured finally. 'Two years ago when I almost died.'

'Ah, yes,' the guru responded. 'A near-death experience. That is different, however. You were there by yourself and then were suddenly confronted by people who had left their physical bodies, people you knew?'

'That's exactly right,' John said, wondering if there was any limit to their mentor's knowledge.

'The difference between then and now,' the guru continued, 'is that two years ago you only arrived at the gate and were not allowed to go through. Today I took you *beyond* the gate, to a place from which none would have returned to their physical bodies without my help. You need have no fear of death while you are on this planet. Just remember this experience.'

'But how do you give us these experiences?' another man asked. 'What's the secret?'

'There is no secret,' the guru replied patiently. 'It is the result of many spiritual lives. There are many Holy Men and each one has a particular gift or gifts to inspire those who seek enlightenment. When one is enlightened, the question becomes the answer. Look no further at this time. Only accept.'

'May I introduce myself?' a lady asked, her eyes shining. 'My name is Margaret. What I have experienced here today has changed my life. How can I go from here and convince others of all the things I have seen?'

'Trying to make others believe is wrong,' he answered firmly. 'The best way to go about it is to relate your experiences and leave it at that. If others wish to accept your words then it will change their lives as well. If they do not, their lives will be poorer, but you should never attempt to brainwash anyone or persuade them by force. In spiritual matters, everyone develops in their own time, during many lifetimes.'

'I'd like to know about my previous lives,' Margaret said. 'How would I go about it?'

'It would be a useless experiment,' the guru told her calmly. 'The sum total of what you have been – good and bad – is what you are now.'

'I'd still find it interesting,' she said defensively.

'Regression is not necessarily truth,' he answered. 'Genetic memories become mixed with the sum total of our own minds and it is very difficult to separate our memories from previous lives from those of our ancestors.' He went on to explain that each of them had to pay the price of their ancestors' actions and the damage they had done to their psyches. 'This whole area is so complicated,' he continued, 'that it is better left alone. Simplify your life. Do not deliberately complicate it. Through your own progression, you will negate the damage that has been done and the efforts you make will be on record. All is known.'

Margaret nodded, accepting his advice, and the guru turned to a young lady sitting at the front of the group.

'I would like to help you,' he said quietly. 'Tell us your name.'

'My name is Lisa,' she replied, 'but I don't think anyone can help me. I have been blind since birth.' She paused, then added, 'I came to listen and to learn. Although I cannot see with my physical eyes, I can see quite clearly with my mind's eye, and I have marvelled at the things that have happened today. Maybe, because I'm seeing with mind instead of brain, I can see colour as it really is. I have much to be thankful for.' She thought for a moment and then said, 'If I could ask for anything it would be for patience. Most of the time I'm impatient with myself and others. It complicates my life.'

'Yes,' the guru said, laughing with her. 'Patience really is a virtue, but very few of us are virtuous,' then he added, 'I think you have to learn to be patient with yourself first. It is impossible to improve any kind of relationship until that same problem has been overcome in ourselves. I can only offer advice. Don't expect too much of yourself. You have had to overcome many obstacles and are anxious to overcome many more, but I believe you are expecting too much too soon. Pace yourself, take stock of your achievements and reward yourself with time – time to relax, to meditate, to think.' He laughed again. 'We have all the time in the Universe, after all. Mind is everlasting. No matter how we hurry in this life, it will make little impact on our spiritual nature as a whole unless we achieve progress.' He smiled once more. 'Please slow down. Enjoy your life and you will find that patience will be your reward.'

'Thank you,' Lisa said. 'I'll do my best.'

'That is all one can ask for,' the guru stated. 'And if your best is not as good as someone else's, it makes no difference in the scheme of things. The only thing that matters is that it is *your* best.'

'I will tell you a story. When I was a young man, I studied spiritual matters with my guru, a great teacher. He asked me to do certain things that, in my opinion, were a waste of time. "Look at the stars," he used to say. "Wonder at them." I did not want to look at the stars, I wanted to be a great teacher, and I told him so, but it made no difference. "I want you to look at the stars and wonder at them because they no longer exist." I laughed then, for I had such admiration for this man, but he was trying to tell me I could see things which no longer existed! My guru continued, "Some of the stars which you see shining so brightly burned out long ago, but as their light does not reach us for hundreds of years, we are seeing an illusion. This dimension is a dream world; there is no reality here. Only when we finally escape from the prison of our physical bodies will we find reality."' The guru paused, watching the faces of his audience.

'It has taken me many years to understand his words, but they are true. Only when we are working with the outer regions of our minds are we in touch with reality. The lower regions are but shadows. In time, you will know this for yourselves but, in the meantime, remember what I have said when you find yourself taking life too seriously.'

'Spiritually advanced people are so relaxed and peaceful,' Lisa responded, 'because they are in touch with reality and know that is the only truth. But most of us find all this extremely difficult to understand.'

'All will be known,' the guru replied placidly. 'It is enough for now that you can think about this and know the truth. I am only asking for your acceptance.'

A young man, who had clearly been waiting to speak for some time, introduced himself.

'My name is Robert and I travelled for two weeks to get here,' he announced. 'I haven't been disappointed and I thank you from the bottom of my heart. I have only one question. Have you ever regretted the path you have taken? It seems to me to be a very lonely existence and you have very few possessions. Don't you feel great sorrow that you are always the giver? You must surely need to receive sometimes to sustain you in this dimension.'

'I chose this path many years ago,' the guru answered. 'I would not know any other life. I give what I can, but I know that I need to give more. I will do so in time, but there is no hurry. As I said before, I can only take people along at their own pace. But I also receive much. I not only receive great love from my audiences but I am sustained by the Source. How could I be lonely?

'As for possessions, I have few because I have no need of them. As you progress spiritually, you will begin to view possessions as clutter – clutter that clouds the mind and spirit. This, of course, will come to you in your own time and if you do not reach that point before you leave this dimension, it does not matter. There is all the time in the Universe. And it may take many lifetimes to learn the most basic lessons.'

'Is love so important?' Robert asked.

'It is the most powerful link you can have with other dimensions,' the guru replied. 'It is your password. Many of you have known physical love, the love of friendship and the love one feels towards children. The love I am speaking about is unconditional love.

'Even when you touch the other dimensions as we have done today, you are still nowhere near the answers. Yet the power is so obvious and the rewards so great that we endeavour to reach out, to be in touch with our souls. And to do this we must love ourselves – and to love ourselves we must have self-respect. For that, our houses must be in order and the first step in achieving that is to have principles and to keep to them. Only then, when you have found peace within yourself and an inner calm, will you also find happiness. You will find – perhaps for the first time – that you will take pleasure in your own company.

'In this materialistic world, people do not love themselves. The majority have spent their lives longing to love others and then wonder why things go very wrong. Sexual love is not what we are discussing here. That is very fleeting. *Pure* love of self gives you self-respect and an ability to live without unnecessary possessions. It enables you to think clearly and concisely and to do what is right for you in an unselfish way. The greatest benefit of all is to be able to give so much to others and remain true to yourself.'

'What exactly is pure love?' a woman named Linda asked.

'It is ecstasy.'

'How do you recognize ecstasy?' Linda went on.

'Waves of energy caress the physical body,' the guru replied, appearing to hesitate for the first time. 'As though enfolding it in a timeless sphere. Yet one is also in a state of unawareness. It is very difficult to explain, but once you have experienced it, it is unforgettable.'

'What are the first steps?' she asked.

'Finding your true self,' he replied promptly. 'It is

usually hidden beneath a façade, but the easiest way to find it is to be truthful to yourself. In our hearts we know when we are lying to ourselves. Lies follow lies and it is almost impossible to extricate yourself from the misery that follows. I am sure that, at some time or another, all of you have asked someone to stop lying to themselves – and experienced utter frustration when they apparently wished to continue. Truth and love are inseparable.

'If you are already enmeshed in a maze of deception but you want to escape, ask yourself innumerable questions and really think about the answers. Truth will eventually prevail. The first ten questions will be the most difficult. After you have answered those truthfully, the process will become easier as time goes on.'

'What are the first ten questions?' another woman asked.

'They will be different for each person depending on their circumstances at the time,' the guru replied. 'You are already making life difficult for yourself by assuming that there are ten special questions. You can start by listing questions about yourself, your motives and behaviour and your life, and then put them in order of priority.'

'I suppose we all expect these things to be special,' the woman said, 'when it's only common sense.'

'You are correct,' he responded. 'However, few people have common sense because they do not apply logic.'

'But . . .' she began, then hesitated. 'I hope you don't think I'm stupid,' she went on, 'but if one is illogical, how can one become logical? It seems too difficult.'

'It is difficult,' the guru agreed, 'but not impossible when approached in the correct manner. For instance, if you are dealing with a problem which concerns several people then it is possible that you are angry with some of them – and this anger makes logical thought very difficult.

So concentrate on the others. Approach the solution from their perspective. Without anger you will be able to think more clearly and feel happier with your logic.

'When you are making decisions which do not involve others, then you must ask yourself questions and think very carefully before you answer them. Know that you have applied truth.

'In either case, if you are not completely logical, at least you will know that you have not been completely illogical and that a certain balance has been maintained. There is no easy way to logic, but this is the easiest way to practise. I assure you that it works, in time, and it brings you face-to-face with yourself. It will be a revelation and will bring many rewards.'

The guru's words had obviously struck a chord with another member of his audience, and she spoke up eagerly as he finished.

'I've applied these measures myself,' she told her companions. 'At first I couldn't face the truth about myself, but gradually I became fascinated by the answers. It was as though I was standing outside myself and listening to a stranger. And eventually, when the stranger became myself, I felt happier than at any time in my life.'

A man who was sitting further back, whose name was Bob, had been nodding in agreement as she spoke.

'It's true that it can be very painful,' he said, 'but the rewards are so great. The experience I had was like being reborn. I can't say that I rediscovered myself, because I had never known my real self.'

'Know yourself and all will be made known to you,' the guru told them. 'Spiritual rewards can be great but they will depend upon your soul. There is no question of winning them by mental debate. You either deserve them at a spiritual level or you do not.'

'I know that's true!' Bob exclaimed, laughing. 'I've had many rewards, but it took a long time. I tried to debate with the powers that be, and my life seemed to get worse until I realized that *expecting* rewards was not at all spiritual. Now I know who I am and where I want to go – and my talent as an artist has improved considerably. I'm in touch with myself.'

'Not only with yourself,' the guru commented. 'You are also linking in with like minds, other artists in this and other dimensions who are on the same path as yourself.

'Always remember that energy attracts like to like. When you look at a blank canvas you are relaxed and your mind energy expands, linking up with like talents. Your thoughts about the painting will actually impregnate the canvas and, even though you will change the energy pattern once you apply the paints, the basis of the composition will always be there. The interaction with other energies and minds will go on for ever.

'Why do you think that the works of the Great Masters attract so much attention hundreds of years after they were created? It is because the mind of the artist is still impregnated in the canvas, and so by looking at or being near the original canvas you can feel that same energy that was left there all those years ago. Once you know how it is left behind in all objects, then you will have a greater understanding of the meaning of life.'

At this point, another lady, who had not contributed to the discussion earlier, made her first comment.

'That's why inanimate objects retain memories, isn't it?' she said. 'I've known psychics who can hold a piece of jewellery and relate personal incidents about its owners, both past and present. They could also describe places where the objects had been.'

'You are correct, of course,' the guru agreed, 'and

although we are talking about very basic things here, it is a beginning. Why is a Stradivarius violin so expensive? First of all because it was made with love, the most magical ingredient of all. Secondly, because of the mind of the artist who made it and, finally, because of the love, artistry and musicianship of all those who have played upon it over the decades.

'Until the whole world has an understanding of such basic knowledge, we can only progress very slowly. It is our spiritual duty to make these things known to others, but you must allow them to absorb it at their own pace. Never force the issue. Those who wish to learn will come back for more – and the seeds of knowledge can grow even on stony ground.

'Nothing is ever as it seems,' the guru exclaimed, smiling at an old memory. 'Many years ago, I was asked to speak to a group of adolescents. It was an inspiring evening, except for one boy who kept interrupting anyone who asked a question. I asked him if he would like to speak at length as he had so much to say for himself, but he laughed and said some of the questions were so stupid that he wanted them to think before they spoke. But after that he quietened down and the rest of the evening was more peaceful.

'Twenty years later I met this man again. He had become a very successful politician, and hated the constant interruptions when he had something important to say. He now regretted his behaviour that evening and realized that, no matter how stupid the questions seemed, they were important to those who asked them. He admitted that he had indeed reaped what he had sown – and that is true for all of us. It is Universal Law.

'Every thought we have goes forth and joins like thoughts, but eventually the collective thoughts return to the originator. It is more pleasant to have love, compassion and unselfishness return than hatred, jealousy and greed.'

'If our thoughts attract like to like and return to us, what happens to the people whose thoughts we have collected?' someone asked. 'Surely they can't return to all of us.'

'They do not return to everyone at the same time,' the guru replied. 'Usually, negative thoughts return when we are at our lowest ebb, when the impact on our psyche will be greater and the lesson harder.'

'That doesn't seem fair somehow,' Miriam put in. 'Quite a lot of people can't stand the strain.'

'It would be convenient if our negative thoughts returned when we are strong,' he answered, 'but the impact would then be negligible. The lesson would be wasted. Universal Law is order. There must be order in all things, and we humans are less than a speck of dust in that order. Universal matters are treated as a whole and not individually, and if something is upsetting the pattern, it will be dealt with.'

There was silence for a time as they all considered the guru's words. Some of them began to wonder if the audience was over, but then he spoke again, asking them to close their eyes once more. As soon as they obeyed, a humming noise filled the cave. A few people opened their eyes again.

'Please keep your eyes closed until I ask you to open them,' the guru requested. 'Otherwise the light will hurt you.'

The uncanny humming grew stronger, reverberating throughout the chamber. When the guru finally told them to look, the sense of anticipation had reached almost fever pitch. And, as soon as they opened their eyes, it was clear that their mentor had saved his most amazing gift of wonder until last.

Standing beside the guru were two men in long, shimmering robes, one blue, the other silver. Each had some kind of ornament on his head, but these were so brilliant that it was difficult to make out what they were. The men were smiling at the astonished audience, and their eyes shone brightly.

'My friends can only stay for a few moments,' the guru said, 'because of the atmosphere at this level. They come from a great spiritual source. They are pure essence. You will never see their like again in this dimension – and you will never be the same again because now you know that all things are possible.' He paused, but no-one spoke. 'Please close your eyes now and do not open them until I ask you.'

After a while the humming ceased and the guru told them to open their eyes. The visitors had gone.

'They are my helpers,' the guru explained briefly. 'I will join them when I leave this planet.' The prospect was obviously pleasing to him. 'You have been greatly honoured,' he added. 'They do not always arrive when I wish them to. And now, my friends, this meeting must come to a close. I thank you all for visiting me.'

The guru pointed to a small bowl on the carpet beside him.

'When I leave, partake of this rice,' he said. 'I give it to you with my blessings.'

With that, he stood up, bowed to the gathering and walked from the cave. No-one moved for a few moments, but then they began to move nearer to the bowl.

'But there are so many of us,' someone said doubtfully. 'There won't be enough.'

'We'll have to take one grain each,' another suggested.

As soon as the words were spoken, the bowl started to fill with rice, spilling over to the floor. Soon, everyone was taking turns to accept handfuls of rice, but as they did so, the bowl filled again and again.

All of the people were astounded, glancing at each other and then back at the overflowing bowl in wonderment. They began to smile and knew, by some silent agreement, that there would never be a time like this again.

Not in their lifetimes.

PART SIX

EMOTIONS

20

Love at First Sight

Love at first sight is the most mind-blowing of all mind waves.

Some scientists believe that the personalities of the two people involved triggers off a chemical reaction in the brain. But the brain cannot function without the stimulation of the thought. The thought is a mind action. In other words, the brain is the computer and the mind is the charge, rather like electricity. When the mind leaves the body at death, the brain dies.

However, I believe the mind-blowing reaction of love at first sight is due to the recognition of someone that one has known in a previous life. That recognition alters the brain chemistry. Everyone who has fallen in love at first sight has been an unconscious alchemist – fusing two minds together as one. They share the same thoughts, the same desires. Wives, husbands, children, family and friends – all are pushed to one side. They cease to exist. Common sense and loyalty to others mean nothing at all.

As a healer and a medium I have been able to help most of the people who came to me in this state, not by solving their problems, but simply by being there when the situation became unbearable. Which it inevitably does.

If the couple are free to love, then it can take its course. The experience, however, is never easy, unless, of course, it eventually calms down and leads to a more unselfish love. After a while, if there are no obsessional ties on either side, each may be able to release a part of their mind that has become so fused with the other. In fact, for the relationship to be happy, it is absolutely necessary that this should happen. Nobody can be that attached for long without losing their independence and freedom of thought.

One young lady asked for my help because she was completely out of control. She worked with a young man, and they had fallen in love as soon as they had set eyes upon each other. For ten months they had both neglected their jobs as they lived each moment only for each other. They had completely blotted out the whole world.

Now her boyfriend had lost his job and she was in danger of losing her own. She was in a desperate situation as they shared a flat and the rent was extremely high.

She told me that she could not possibly go back to live with her parents as she hadn't seen very much of them in the past ten months. She also felt that she had matured and thought that her parents would still treat her as a child.

She said, 'I can't understand what has happened to me. My parents have tried to contact me several times at work, and when I return their call I only have a few words to say to them. Although I still love them, it is as if they are strangers. I have nothing in common with them any more. We used to be such good friends. I know it isn't their fault, but the gulf between us widened so quickly.

'My boyfriend and I are still very much in love, but it seems to have destroyed the rest of my life. I feel guilty all the time.'

I tried to explain what had happened to her. That it really wasn't anybody's fault – it was a whim of nature.

After a while, she calmed down. I advised her to take

some action like going to meet her parents, so that she could shed some of the guilt. She agreed. I then advised her to have a mental button to press when she was at work so that she could go into working mode. When she left work she could press the button again, and go into a relaxed mode.

Having a mental button to push is a very easy way of disciplining the mind when one has lost control. When two people are in the 'falling in love at first sight' state, they are completely out of control, although neither party would agree with this at the time. The button method reminds them that they have to discipline their thoughts, and is extremely effective.

After she had left, I thought about all the people, young and old, who had come to me with the same problem. I felt very sorry for them, having been through the same thing myself. No-one can possibly understand the heights and depths of this kind of relationship unless they have experienced it for themselves. One minute you think you are in heaven, the next in hell.

The young woman contacted me again two weeks later. They had both visited her parents, who had been delighted to see them. After hearing of their dilemma, they offered to pay their rent until the boyfriend had found alternative employment. 'We didn't want to take their money,' she told me 'but they insisted. We have promised to return the money to them as soon as we can possibly do so.

'Betty, I am feeling so much better and not so guilty, but I am still having trouble with the button,' she laughed. 'My boyfriend is more successful at it than I am. I felt quite annoyed when he told me he could turn me off.'

I told her that he would probably be more successful with his next job because he was able to do this.

Her boyfriend found another job, and *was* very successful, but she was so jealous of him working with someone other than herself that she eventually destroyed the relationship.

She later married and had two children. When speaking about her experience she said, 'It was pure heaven and pure hell all at the same time. The person I am with now is warm, loving and totally unselfish. I still have a lot to learn, but I am more peaceful.'

The problem one usually has with the 'falling in love at first sight' syndrome is that when it fizzles out on one side only, you have a situation where obsession and hatred take over, propelling both sides into a nightmare situation. I will discuss this in following chapters.

Perhaps there are those of you who have never fallen in love at first sight, and who believe that this situation would never arise in your life, that you would be sensible and keep any relationship in check. If it happens to you, believe me, you would be as helpless as everyone else.

What happens? What is it that makes normally sensible people so destructive of their careers and home life?

From the previous chapters, you will know that mind energy is extremely potent. It invades everything.

This syndrome is different. It is a fusion of mind energies that have the same vibrational level. Everything is vibration, and when you have two that are identical, it reinforces the weaknesses, the strengths, and particularly the needs of those two people.

Something else also enters the arena – and that is romance. Most women would give anything for a really romantic relationship. Forget the sex, that is really only a small part of it. Perhaps not for the first few months, but certainly if there is to be a relationship that is going to last.

That is why many young girls love to be with older men

and vice-versa. If one part of the whole has experience, then they know that romance has to become 90 per cent of the relationship. When the romance has gone the relationship ceases to exist.

I do not believe that the majority of men or women realize what an integral part of the relationship romance must be. It must also be genuine, because one knows instinctively when it is not.

There is a time in everyone's life when they are ready for such an experience. Relationships and marriages are never easy, unless you have been extremely lucky or you are duping yourself.

We are all unique to ourselves. There will never be anyone like us again, not even if we return – because by then, hopefully, we would have progressed. We all have hopes, desires and needs. If you happen to meet someone with the same feelings, and their mind wave vibrations are on your exact wavelength, the fusion can happen without you even needing to speak to or touch that person.

Although your uniqueness will always be preserved, you will, for as long as the relationship lasts, feel as one person.

The need to be with that person all of the time becomes obsessive. It is at this stage that you forget the people that have previously meant so much to you.

This kind of love is really a type of illness; it can become extremely debilitating, and yet you are unable to walk away from it. Indeed, you do not wish it to end, ever. It is like a drug, and the more that you can get the better.

Another lady who had fallen into this syndrome asked for my help. Unfortunately, in this case, she was married with two small children.

She had met a friend's husband whilst he was delivering his children to school. She told me, 'We just smiled at each other, and my legs gave way, my heart started to pound and I felt dizzy. He came over and asked me if I was OK and would I like a coffee. We drove to the nearest coffee shop and parked our cars outside. After we had sat down and he had ordered, he said, "Has the same thing that has happened to me happened to you?" I stared at him with my mouth open. I must have looked like a fish out of water. "What do you mean?" I asked. He smiled. "I mean the heart pounding and the shaky legs." I was speechless. I could not believe that it had happened to both of us. I still can't.'

She went on to tell me the whole story – the excitement, the passion, the romance. Stolen hours when they both should have been elsewhere. What she could not come to terms with were the lies.

'I have never lied to my husband or my mother, yet here I am telling lies as though I have had a lifetime of experience. He is doing the same with his wife and family. We are both guilt-ridden, but we cannot part. We have tried, but it is useless. It is as though he has taken over my soul.'

She did not know how right she was. They were both in possession of a large portion of each other's mind.

I have listened to so many stories which follow exactly the same pattern, and the outcome is very rarely happy.

I tried to help, but their obsession was too great and they pursued it to the bitter end, breaking up both families. Finally, when they both let go, they were left alone with their shattered memories.

When I asked her whether it had been worth it, she smiled and said, 'Yes it was, and I will have my memories for ever. Maybe, one day, it will happen again.' That is always the hope, of course, but it very rarely does.

Many people never fall in love at first sight in their lives. Those that have never forget it, and very rarely regret it, even though they have suffered the most terrible physical and mental traumas.

When minds have been fused in this fashion there is a mind energy link that never breaks. One has only to think of that person, and it is as though all the bad times never happened and you are back at the beginning. Memories, though, can preserve the sanity with reminders of the bad times.

It is easy to understand how crimes of passion are committed. Imagine, after the fusing of two minds, one half of the partnership wishes to escape, perhaps through an instinctive sense of self-preservation, or through information acquired through mind transference, when all things are known.

The partner who is being rejected has become hooked on the relationship; as I have mentioned before, being in this state is like having regular injections of a very powerful drug. When the drug is refused, it can lead to temporary insanity, and in this state a murder can be committed. The person who commits the crime is usually in an out-of-the-body state, and very often does not remember anything. Crimes of passion are recognized in France, where they are far more sympathetic to them than we are in this country.

Is there any way at all of breaking the hold of this sort of obsession when it happens to you?

I believe the only way one can deal with it is to move away. This releases the mind link a little, though not much. However, if you do not see that person for a number of years, then it does, eventually, weaken. I will not say die – for it never dies. You cannot kill off the part of someone's mind that has been left behind – it will be with you for ever. What you *can* do is weaken its hold by not having any contact.

If it is impossible to move, then you must make up your mind never to see that person again.

I remember one man, who came to see me in a terrible dilemma. He loved his wife but had fallen in love at first sight with another woman. He did not wish to be disloyal to his wife but could not keep away from the other woman.

His guilt was making him ill. 'It is not as though I am having a sexual relationship with her,' he said. 'I'm not. I just want to be with her. What is it that makes me feel like this when I know I love my wife?'

I talked to him for an hour explaining the fusion, and how it affects the chemistry of the brain. 'You will have to stop seeing her or you will lose everything,' I said.

His reply was to be expected. 'I can't do that. Not at the moment. Perhaps later I will be able to do so?' I assured him that it would be too late, and reminded him that the kind of love he had for his wife was normal. The feelings he had for the other woman – wonderful though they were – were not.

He continued to see the other woman until his wife became suspicious. He was so frightened of losing her that he decided, once and for all, not to see the other woman again. He had made up his mind, and that was going to be the end of it.

Unfortunately the mistress, which by this time she had become, had other ideas. She had become hooked on the drug and did not want the relationship to end. He was pursued until finally he had to move.

Needless to say, his wife found out, and although they stayed together, their relationship was never the same.

No-one was really guilty or innocent – only victims.

It is not for any one of us to judge. This fusion of minds is a very simple process. It is instantaneous and can happen at any time to anyone, no matter what their age. If you are in your seventies and believe that it cannot happen to you, don't be too sure.

The next chapter is about an equally selfish love – young love.

21

Young Love

The majority of teenagers are selfish, especially when they meet and fall in love for the first time. In this chapter I am referring to ordinary love, the kind of love that takes time to develop. It may be several months before it becomes apparent to the two people concerned that they are in love. However, when it eventually dawns on them, they want to live only for each other. Family, friends and career all suffer.

Who can blame them? After all, falling in love for the first time is perhaps the most wonderful emotional experience one can have. But friends become aggrieved at being left out. Parents worry all the time about the sexual aspect, about AIDS in particular. They also worry about unwanted babies, especially as they are probably enjoying a freedom they had forgotten whilst their children were growing up, and have no wish to be propelled into the nightmare of nappies and sleepless nights again.

Neither do they wish to counsel a teenage mother whose boyfriend has now left the scene. Some stay in such circumstances, but many are too young to cope. Parents of young men who are about to become fathers may find that their son is suffering from depression and guilt. It is never easy for either set of parents to cope with the consequences.

However, whilst the love affair is in its prime it is

wonderful for those who are in love. The unhappiness and worry experienced by those around them is ignored.

Can adults help to ease the situation? Only by giving the couple leaflets about AIDS and other sexually transmitted diseases, by providing a list of the cost of bringing up a child unaided and, as far as possible, giving them all the facts of life and living.

Well, you can try. My experience has been that they will not read the leaflets. They will insist that their partner has never been with anyone else and that none of the facts will apply to them. For the sake of the sensible teenagers who *will* listen, parents and friends must persevere.

The old saying that 'you can never put an old head on young shoulders' is absolutely correct. When parents ask their children to be careful, they are usually looked upon as being old-fashioned.

Most of the time, parents would like to get on with their own lives. After all, when their children have grown up, they can have a new start, with a career, a hobby, or just being able to meet their friends and relax.

In my capacity as a medium and healer I have heard the same stories over and over again. They do not change. Most parents cannot believe that it is happening to them.

I remember my own mother, left to bring up three teenagers alone, begging us to be careful when we met our boyfriends in the evenings. She asked us so often that we ignored her, believing her to be over-anxious and old-fashioned.

I repeated the very same words to my own children, who listened with only one ear. Now they are in the same position, repeating the same worn-out sentence.

If you are in this position whilst reading this book, take heart, you are not alone. Millions of people are sharing the same experience with you.

There are some unselfish young people about, and perhaps your son or daughter will be lucky enough to meet one of them.

One young man told me that he lived for the nights that he and his girlfriend shared together. 'We had a tremendous sexual attraction for each other,' he said. 'One day I could see that she looked really tired, and I asked her if she was ill. It was only after questioning her again and again that she told me the truth – that our love-making was wearing her out. She said that she had felt she couldn't discuss it with me, and was frightened that I would leave her.'

He was really upset. 'How could she think that? Didn't she know I loved her for herself and not for that alone?' I suggested that perhaps he had never told her. He admitted that he hadn't. He held his head in his hands. 'I can't believe how selfish I have been. I really love that girl.'

They are now very happily married.

That was a happy ending. But young men, on the whole, can be very selfish, with physical feelings leading them on to pastures new all the time. When they should be giving their all to a career or study, their minds conjure up pictures of new conquests, and they do not care who they hurt in the process.

Fortunately, they also require money. Having to work hard to have money is their great saviour, and sanity gradually prevails in most cases.

I have had many conversations with men about their emotional problems, and it is enlightening to hear how many of them have terrible guilt feelings about the girls they used in their teens. It seems in most cases to have brought them face-to-face with themselves.

Young girls can also be extremely selfish and equally sexy, but they are not as a rule quite so sexually athletic, and are more inclined to be romantic. Generally they are not as ruthless as their male counterparts.

Most people put it all down to hormones, but if that was the whole problem, then every male and female would be the same. Fortunately they are not.

The major culprit in all this – though not in any way a wicked one – is the mind energy itself. When we are young and energetic, we are usually extremely positive, even if our ideas are positively wrong. As you now know, positivity expands the mind *ad infinitum*. This opens the chakras and meridian lines so that even more life-force is absorbed, which keeps the body in an extremely healthy condition, and also stimulates hormone activity. It is true to say that it is all in the mind.

The problems we have to face with career, marriage, children or just surviving, draw the mind energy in, and the chakras begin to slow down. This affects the hormones, which in turn has a calming effect on the sexual appetite.

That is when we have time to think and to ponder. It also allows the higher mind to become part of our thinking. It is at this point that we find out whether we can have genuine unselfish feelings about our partners and others.

Some of us pass the test, but others do not.

We all start out as rough diamonds. To gain character, humility, generosity, and to love unselfishly, every facet of the diamond has to be polished. The polishing process is extremely painful but the result, the final jewel, is well worth the effort.

The best advice I can pass on to parents and friends who are trying to cope with teenage love is – always be there for them. No matter how much grief and despair they bring into our lives they are our children.

A secure home with a loving family can give young lovers a sense of responsibility, but most of all a base where they can retreat when things get out of hand.

Unselfish love is the greatest healer of all.

22

Unselfish Love

Within a Relationship

This is a very rare kind of love. If you have it, hold on to it for ever.

It is about people thinking of others first, of the joys of giving instead of receiving. These people never allow the romance to die within a relationship. They are able to transform the dullest of days into something warm and wonderful.

No matter how old, plain or fat you are, they make you believe that you are a prince or princess. That is all it needs for you to take an interest in yourself, to diet and look young again. If nobody cares, why make the effort.

Of course we all like to look nice, but there is a more powerful incentive when you know that it is going to be appreciated.

The mind waves that flow in such a relationship are gentle and caressing and this can only be achieved when the love is genuine.

Unselfish lovers are the kind that no-one ever wants to leave. I have often heard people say they wished they could die first as they would not wish to live without their partner. They know that the love they have received would be very hard to find again with someone else.

Most important, the romance of this kind of love never dies. The more unselfish one is, the longer it can be kept alive.

Being aware of the needs of your partner, without having to ask, is most important, and requires a tremendous amount of sensitivity.

Sex is not the driving force in this kind of relationship. As well as romance, warmth and companionship are the main considerations. A warm hug from someone who loves you dispels a multitude of negative emotions, and simply knowing that you are receiving such love is a prevention against many ills which begin in the mind. The knowledge that you will be cared for if you are sick helps to keep negativity at bay and ensures a healthier existence.

Being able to bestow upon someone a feeling of self-worth is an incredible achievement.

There is only one problem. Unselfish people are used and abused by society in general. If you have an unselfish partner, try to return their love and to support them in turn.

Most important of all, share the excess of your love with others.

Unselfish Love for Others

There are people all over the world who put into practice the unselfish love they have for others. These people do not seek reward of any kind. They are there to serve.

Charities have very few paid members – most are volunteers who give up their precious time for a cause. Those who work with handicapped children give of their time, freely and willingly, and are rewarded with trust from their charges.

Mentally handicapped children give so much love. They live by their instincts; some of them are able to link into the Universal Mind and become remarkable achievers. There are those who have extraordinary gifts. Some can remember any piece of music once it has been heard and play it back faultlessly on the piano, without ever having any lessons. One young man can instantly tell you which day relates to any date in any year you like to mention. Others achieve fame with their paintings.

The gifts of these savants would be lost to the world without the love and the scope to progress provided by their parents and helpers. It takes time and patience to recognize that a child has a special talent.

I believe that these talented children have a direct link with Universal Knowledge. They are able to pick up the waves with their mind, and once this mind link has been made all they have to do is tap the source.

The volunteers who deliver meals-on-wheels to old people unable to fend for themselves are another example of this type of unselfish love. These volunteers are people who could quite easily stay at home with a good book, yet their efforts go unrecognized most of the time.

Groups of people all over the world are spending their spare time trying to save the environment.

Every day, ordinary people are giving their time to make someone else happy.

There are those who are dedicated but who receive a wage for their services. Little is known of the work they do in their own time for which they are not paid. Teachers, for instance, have to check homework in their own time. When they should be relaxing at home, they are sur-rounded by piles of work. They also give time for the preparation of school plays and musicals, for sports and a host of other things. They do this willingly and give unselfishly. I do not believe that many parents are aware of this.

Nurses do not take up their career for the salaries they receive, but are dedicated to caring for others. They should have a decent living wage, and more. They often work far beyond the hours they are paid for because they are concerned about a patient, and their unselfish love has been taken advantage of for so many years.

Many of them know about mind waves because they have to work at night and see so many people die in the early hours when they are at their lowest ebb. Nurses have told me that they have seen spirits sitting or standing by the bed of the person who is dying. When the person dies the spirit disappears. One young woman said that it was as though they had come to take them away. She was absolutely right, of course, although she knew nothing about spiritualism.

I used to live very near a hospital, and ten of the nurses would come and visit me. They had nearly all seen a spirit or knew someone that had seen one. That is why they sought me out; to ask questions and find out why the spirits were there.

I would also put doctors into this unselfish category. They care for their patients even though they are so overworked that they have little time to spend in conversation.

Priests are extremely caring people, and spend many unpaid hours looking after their parish. Night and day, whatever the weather, they are there giving their love to those in need.

I must not ignore those who are practising alternative methods of healing. The majority are not paid at all and yet they give of their time, their love and their insight.

They are usually left out of official lists of commendations so I am making quite sure they are included in mine.

I am quite sure that I have left out a host of other people who give unselfishly of their time. I hope you will all forgive me.

When one works in an atmosphere of giving it is far easier to give unselfish love than it is to commit oneself on a one-to-one basis.

Parents

Parents should not be forgotten. Where would we be without our parents? Most parents give unselfish love to their children all of their lives. Even when the children have left home, their parents never stop worrying about them.

This is not just a mind link, it is a genetic link as well. Telepathy between parents and children is not uncommon; the mind is somehow linked at soul level.

It is said that we reincarnate in groups. For instance, your father could have been your son in a previous life, your mother a sister, your brother a husband. There is no doubt that there are family groups who are so close that they are almost one.

Parents are often used and abused, but they accept it as part and parcel of parenthood – which is just as well, because children can be very thoughtless, even when they are middle-aged. It is only when they themselves become parents that they appreciate their own. Alas, it is sometimes too late.

One word of warning. Do not become too unselfish with your children. It is necessary for them to learn how to give also.

If you happen to be a selfish person, it is possible to

change. Offer to help within the home, try looking at the situation from the other person's point of view, but most important of all, stop thinking about yourself – you may find other people more interesting.

23

Hate

Hate is totally destructive, both to the person who is giving out such vibrations and to the one who is receiving them. There can be no happy outcome; it is a futile emotion.

Alas, there is much of it about, and it is very often justified. The hurt that it causes is very real; one's whole body feels as though it has been crunched up inside. Why does it feel like this?

When you hate, you are using your imagination in such a way that it stands to reason your mind waves will connect with like mind waves.

The spirit world is not occupied solely by saintly mind waves; it has its share of rogues and evil-minded people just as we have in this world. Whatever you are at your death, you will continue to be until *you* decide to change. Hence all the negative minds that can't wait to attach themselves to you, thus strengthening the negativity in your own mind.

A young man who came to me for clairvoyance had been carrying on a hate campaign for eighteen months. He told me that a former business colleague had smeared his reputation whilst he was looking after company business abroad. When he returned, he found that he had been replaced by this man. He asked for my help.

Whilst we were sitting together I was taken back in time

and was given a clear picture of how Universal Law had been triggered into action. From the information I received, it became obvious to me that the young man with me was not a saint in any sense of the word. He had connived at the downfall of the man who had previously held his job. It was, quite simply, a case of an eye for an eye.

When I explained this to him he was not at all pleased at having been found out. I told him, 'When you visit a medium you must expect to come face-to-face with yourself. Whether it is information from the past, the future or survival evidence, the truth will become known.'

He sat, head bowed, and did not speak for a while. Then he said, 'I had completely forgotten my part in having my predecessor sacked. But you are correct.'

I tried to explain Universal Law to him, although at the time I thought it was falling on deaf ears. He had so much hate inside him that his mind energy was muddied, not the usual bright white light – which is always a sign of outside negative influences.

I advised him to look to the future and visualize the kind of life that he would be willing to work toward. I asked him to remove himself, physically, from the person he hated, to ensure that he did not accidentally bump into him. And, above all, not to follow him around as he had been doing. This is a dangerous act at the best of times. When one is full of hate it could lead to violence on both sides.

Clairvoyantly, I could see a very bright future for him in spite of the fact that he was currently in the depths of despair. I gave him this information, but I still didn't think he was listening to me. When he left I presumed that I would never see him again.

Three months later, he called and asked for an appointment. He was a totally different human being. He looked extremely attractive, smartly dressed and happy. He told me that his mind had blanked out when I had reminded him of his misdeeds. He said, 'To tell you the truth, I didn't want to listen to any more, and hardly heard your words.' I laughed. 'You don't have to tell me that. I was well aware of your thoughts. Tell me, if you weren't listening, what brought about the change? You must have done something pretty drastic.' He stared into my eyes as though he was trying to understand himself. 'It was funny,' he said. 'When I left you, I felt as though I was in a daze and when I got home I went straight to bed, even though it was only three o'clock in the afternoon. I stayed there for two days, sleeping all the time. I only got out of bed to make myself a cup of tea now and again. When I eventually decided to leave my bed it became clear to me that I had been enjoying the hurt. It also occurred to me that there had been a presence around me that had encouraged my feelings of hate. I did as you suggested and visualized my life as I wished it to be [so he must have been listening, after all], without the terrible negative influences, and vowed that I would get rid of the hate and free myself from them. It was tough, but it worked. I can't describe the feeling of peace I had when the hate eventually disappeared. It was as though I had been ill for all those months.'

I assured him that he had been ill. Hate is a terrible emotion, a mental disease.

Imagine waves of black energy being projected towards a person. These waves mingle with that person's mind waves, and at the same time attracts like mind waves of spirit people. This interaction becomes extremely dangerous. The boosted black energies return with a vengeance, rather like a boomerang, hitting the giver head-on. And so it goes on until the waves are no longer being projected. It is only then that they lose their power.

The action taken by this young man had saved his sanity. It is unbelievably difficult to reverse such a process; he had a lot of guts, and was to be admired.

When something awful happens to you, have a few weeks of self-pity if you want but do not allow real hate to enter your life. It is hard, because when one has really been hurt, hate is a wonderful way of trying to return the hurt. But I am afraid that once you indulge yourself in this way the road back is extremely difficult, especially if you have become ill in the process.

It is the same with racial hatred. Everyone involved becomes mentally sick. It does not matter a jot what colour or creed you are, if you indulge in this most horrendous type of hate, then the sickness will hit you sooner or later.

When such hate has spread into a collective unconscious, we hide behind each other when crimes are committed. Hate mind waves are virulent, and will attack anyone that happens to be in their path. That is why many people become involved who have not previously taken part in any act of racial hatred.

It only takes one sick person with a powerful mind to create mass hysteria. Hitler was such a person. He was a very lonely man who had such a hatred of the Jews that he turned a whole nation against them. The concentration camps and gas chambers will never be forgotten.

The hatred between countries and countrymen and between one person and another must be stopped now, or our planet will die. It cannot sustain such hatred. Earth is a living organism, and it will choose the time for its own death. We must all do our part in supporting it. By refusing to have anything to do with hatred, we can help it to survive.

Think love, and ignore hate. It just hates to be ignored!

24

Jealousy

Couples

Jealousy is a destructive emotion. It is an emotion that cannot easily be controlled. I have had to give counselling and healing to both sexes when they have suffered from this and have been out of control. It is not easy.

One man who asked me for help told me that he shook from head to toe every time he thought of his ex-girlfriend going out with another man. He could not control his thoughts or the shaking fits. Consequently, his work suffered, and he was in the difficult position of trying to hold on to his job when he came to see me for the first time.

I gave him healing and explained that if his ex-girlfriend no longer sought his company, then he must let go. There is no longer a relationship when one half does not want to know. My words fell on deaf ears. As soon as I mentioned the lady in question, he shook like a rattle.

I suggested hypnotherapy. He was not interested. Unfortunately, I did not think it would work in his case. For hypnotherapy to be effective, you have to be committed to curing yourself.

I tried to persuade him to see a doctor or psychiatrist, but he didn't want to do this either. In fact, he was not seeking a cure for the jealousy, only his shaking fits.

I am sure that everyone has had pangs, or even long

periods of feeling jealous, but with the support of good friends and family it eventually calms down. Unfortunately, there are people like my patient who suffer the most dreadful physical symptoms brought on by the mental anguish; no matter how hard they try to discipline themselves, the condition will not go away.

It is not a question of willpower.

Heartbreak is one of the reasons that people suffer so much, and believe me, it is a very common condition. The stress and tension put a great strain on the heart muscles, and this causes the sufferer to experience chest pains similar to those of angina.

Of course, it all starts in the mind, and it is the mind that has to be calmed before these symptoms can be cured.

Jealousy is a perfect example of misuse of the imagination. If you remember the rule of Universal Law, whatever you give out must return. It is obvious that by using your imagination in a self-destructive way you will destroy yourself one way or another.

One prime example is to imagine your ex-partner in the arms of someone else. If they have found someone new, or even if they returned to a previous partner, it is quite likely that they may be quarrelling or having silent sessions rather than falling into each other's arms. Masochism is rife when one is feeling hard done by.

Another example is to imagine a conversation that your ex is having with another person, perhaps discussing intimate details of your past sex life. If this is happening, then it is the other person who needs to be pitied for having sunk so low.

By far the worst experience is to actually meet your ex-partner when they are with someone else – especially if they are kissing and cuddling each other. Yes, I know.

You want to throttle them both. But feeling like that only makes matters worse, and really doesn't solve anything. There is still such a thing as freedom of thought and deed, and it applies to all of us. Just because you do not agree with the decision someone has made about their life, doesn't mean they are criminals in any way.

I asked my patient if he would write all his thoughts down on paper every day, and when he had finished to burn them in a ceremonial tin. I have mentioned this therapy in my other books, but I do not think it can be repeated too often. He agreed to do this, and I made an appointment for him to see me again the following week.

When I saw him a week later he told me that he had committed murder on paper every day but that he was feeling better. It was to be twelve months before the extreme symptoms eased, and another six months before he stopped shaking.

I told him that I did not believe he could ever have a successful relationship or marriage until he had conquered the terrible jealousy that had consumed him in his last affair.

Somehow, he managed to control his emotions. He was married five years later, and now has three children, and is extremely happy.

He told me that he uses pen and paper all the time. He feels that by putting his thoughts into words on paper and then burning them, he has kept himself healthy and happy.

There is no doubt that he had been so close to his ex-girlfriend that they had formed a telepathic relationship. That is why he reacted so strongly when he thought about her – he was experiencing a mind-to-mind contact.

I happened to meet the young lady some years later,

quite by accident. She knew that her boyfriend had been to see me at the time of their breakup. She said, 'I knew when he was thinking bad thoughts about me because I used to feel icy cold all over. It would take ages for me to get warm.'

I found this interesting. It is easy to find a spirit when they are in a room because there will be an icy spot. Spirits project their mind energy, hoping they will be seen. The boyfriend was doing exactly the same thing with his mind, albeit unconsciously.

Families

Another kind of jealousy that is very destructive is that experienced in families. Brothers and sisters who are jealous of each other can cause terrible disruption within a family, so much so that it can create a situation where the parents actually divorce because they can no longer bear to live in such an unharmonious atmosphere.

Such a case was brought to my notice by a young friend of mine. He was a very successful hairdresser and had opened three shops in different areas. His brother and sister were jealous of his success, so he asked them if they would like to work for him.

He gave his sister work as a receptionist in one of the shops, and his brother was given the task of keeping another of the shops in a different area clean and well-stocked. He kept them both apart to avoid any further problems.

Unfortunately, at work they telephoned each other frequently, complaining about their wages and conditions; which, incidentally, were good.

At home they argued with him all the time, until eventually he sacked them both and moved out of his home.

The father thought that he had been treating them badly. The mother, who admired her successful son, argued his cause. Eventually the parents separated and Mum went to live with her son. It was all so unnecessary.

If the other children had tried to achieve instead of becoming jealous, the family would probably still be together. After all, the son had spent ten years in his profession and had worked all hours of the day and night to achieve his ambition whilst the others had just wasted their time.

I always try to encourage everyone to achieve something in their lives. Not to impress others, but to have the satisfaction of knowing how *much* they can achieve. How do you know what heights you can reach if you do not try? If the effort is not rewarded by success, try again. We are all unique. We are all capable of achieving. All you have to do is to find the right key.

Many successful people have opened several doors before they have found the correct key, but in their hearts they knew they would eventually succeed.

Never be jealous of other people's success and no matter how young or old you are, never stop trying. If in the end you still do not find the right key, don't despair. Effort is never wasted, and you will have earned the respect of family and friends for never giving up. That in itself is success.

Children

Jealousy is an emotion that must be checked as soon as it is recognized in young children. Otherwise they will become unbearable adults, making their own lives a misery.

Some parents deliberately ignore the signs, especially if

they have a jealous nature themselves. It is never easy to recognize oneself in another, especially if that person is your own child.

There are many ways one can help these children. Pretend to give them a little of their own medicine. If they have a present, show them how jealous you are of that present, make them feel miserable. When you feel that your action has had an effect, point out that you were only pretending so that they could feel the hurt for themselves.

There are children who need love to overcome their problem. Perhaps they believe that their brother or sister, or their father, is receiving more love than they are. This is a very common form of jealousy. If they think that someone in the family is a favourite, and that they are losing out, you may be able to explain that the extra interest is due to the fact that the other child is having a hard time at school, or that their best friend has left them. Perhaps you can explain that extra compassion is needed when someone is suffering. Then end by telling them that at this particular time they themselves obviously need a little extra love and compassion and that you will give it to them.

It would be a good idea also to impress upon them how wonderful it is *not* to be so dependent on receiving love. For there will be times in their lives when they will not be receiving attention from anyone, and that is why they have to grow strong and independent whilst they are children. Point out that one day you, their parent, will need help, and will need their love and support. Such things have to work both ways.

I am sure that intelligent parents can work out a successful formula for their children, but for the sake of all the family, do not ignore the problem.

Jealousy creates terrible atmospheres, wherever it may be. If you have a jealous nature, find your pen and paper and start writing now for your own sake. And keep writing.

25

Envy

Never be envious of anybody. People who appear to have everything very rarely do. Their lives are no different to the lives of those who have very little. They have stress, sickness, emotional upheavals and tragedies and although their material wealth can cushion the effects, it cannot take away the harsh realities of life. I assure you that there is no need to be envious of them. In all walks of life, people have different responsibilities and none of them are easy.

I knew a lady some years ago who appeared to have it all. She was happily married to a banker. They had a wonderful home and three beautiful, gifted children who were all at private schools.

One day her husband had a fatal heart attack on the station platform. All the family were devastated.

To keep her children at school, she sold her home and contents and moved into a flat. Eventually, she had to supplement the little income she had by taking a job as a secretary.

She told me some years later that it had been the making of her children and herself. The tragedy had given her self-respect, and she had found a strength within herself that she had not realized existed.

How many times have we read of the downfall of prominent people in our society who appeared to have everything. Believe me, the higher you get, the harder you fall.

If you want to achieve however, you have tremendous potential which can be released once you have acquired the habit of positive thought. You will have clarity of vision and an intuitive knowing of where you are going and what you can achieve, but do not judge yourself by what you are now because the *new* you will be entirely different. The rewards of positive thought are immense.

Whatever your goal, remember that whoever you hurt on the way up, you will meet on the way down. Those who reach the top at other people's expense are courting disaster. Universal Law – whatever you give out you will receive ten-fold – will always have the last word.

Achieving the correct way involves a tremendous amount of hard work and regard for others. It also requires an intuitive feeling of when to stop – there is no point in going on beyond your natural potential, it will only result in ill health. When your work or play ceases to be enjoyable and becomes a drag, stop there and let others who are less knowing than yourself take the candy at the top – it invariably turns out to be floss.

Envy is something that we should put out of our lives for ever, in a way it is stealing by thought. If it does not belong to you and you cannot achieve it yourself, then forget it!

26

Greed

This must be the most terrible emotion of all. It is destructive and encompasses all others.

Greed has caused the broken hearts of many people who have lost all their life-savings to those they counted as friends.

At the moment it seems that the whole country needs to be on the alert as more and more sophisticated methods are being used to extract money from innocent victims. Be careful if you boast that you will never be caught out; anyone can fall into these sophisticated traps.

I know of many people who have been brought to their knees by the greed of partners, friends or family.

One such person spent twenty-five years of his life building up his business. When his sons were old enough they joined him. His nephew, who was an accountant, asked if he could join them, and as they had just lost an old and trusted friend who had been their company's accountant, they agreed to take him on.

After only three years, the greed of the nephew brought them all down and the company was put into liquidation.

The father could not face starting again and died a broken man.

Why is it that some people believe they have the right to cash in on the hard work of others?

Greed, surely, cannot make a person happy. Greedy

people must always be looking for a way to relieve someone of their hard-earned cash. This in itself is immoral. Fortunately, Universal Law brings its own punishments and no-one escapes – the punishment always fits the crime. It strikes at the weakest moments in one's life. That is why it can sometimes feel as though the punishment far *exceeds* the crime.

How many times have we learned of families who never visited their old and sick relatives whilst they were alive but gathered together as soon as they died. It is sickening to witness such greed. More sickening still is the way in which they fight each other over the will or the contents of the house.

I feel sad when I see old people scrimping and scraping to keep body and soul together, simply because their children have told them how upset they would be if Mum or Dad sells the family home. These people could live comfortably if they sold the family home and lived in a small house or bunaglow, but they are emotionally blackmailed by their children, who want to keep their probable inheritance intact. Having to keep the home clean and in reasonable condition is enough to make these old people ill. But unfortunately, they are made to feel that their children come first.

It is amazing the power that children have over their parents. There are thousands of parents who are absolutely blind to their children's faults. It does not mean that you have to stop loving them – but you must appreciate that they are normal human beings who like to have their own way, if they can. By recognizing their selfishness in the early stages of their life, you can stop them from becoming greedy adults.

One of the first signs in children is when they refuse to share their toys and sweets. Large families tend to be less greedy than smaller units, because there is usually less to go around and they have to share all the time. It is absolutely essential that children are taught to share and that if there is only one sweet left in the packet then they should offer it first to someone else.

There is so much greed about that it makes one feel ashamed of the human race. But the most terrible acts of greed are those that have tragically poisoned our environment and made this planet potentially a living hell.

The Environment

The whole world can see the destruction that has been wrought by greed. For example, the millions of tons of chemicals that have been used so liberally on the land. Those living near farms in some areas are constantly sick when crop spraying time comes around, and the chemicals can also cause further problems later on.

I remember reading about a couple who bought a little cottage on the edge of farmland. They had moved out of a town to get away from the pollution and so that they could grow their own vegetables. They were both vegetarian – so, incidentally, was their dog.

First of all, the dog became ill and died. He had been poisoned. As the dog could not get out of the garden and was always accompanied on its walks, they could not understand how this could have happened.

After a while the lady of the house became crippled with what seemed to be a very bad case of osteo-arthritis. Neither of them could believe their bad luck; after all, they were living a clean healthy life and did not use any poisons or chemicals in their garden. Eventually she died. The postmortem revealed that her body contained large quantities of a chemical used by farmers.

The husband looked at the lie of his land and realized that the farmland sloped down into his garden. The lowest point was the vegetable plot. He took a sample of soil to be tested and it was found to be totally polluted with this particular chemical. He went at once to see the farmer, who was not at all sympathetic, saying that he would continue to use the chemical on his land as it was the cheapest way of controlling pests.

The husband eventually died of liver disease due to his system having been poisoned for so long.

I remember how shocked I was on reading that particular story. Here were two people trying to live as near to nature as possible, supposedly growing their own fresh vegetables, and one greedy man on adjoining land killed them. How greedy can you get?

The farmer was aware that his land reached its lowest point at the bottom of their cottage garden. He was also aware of the enormous quantity of chemicals he was using and that this couple were growing their own vegetables at the lowest drainage point.

There are thousands of people around, not only farmers, who poison the land every minute of every day with some chemical or another. Never mind that children and animals play on this land and that they are liable to become contaminated. Never mind that animals may graze on the same land in years to come. These chemicals cannot be washed from the soil, even by perpetual rain. They are there for ever.

Many animals and birds have been wiped out by chemicals that have been sprayed so liberally in ordinary gardens.

I saw one woman buying up cartons and cartons of slug pellets. I asked her whether she knew these could be dangerous to wildlife and children – what on earth was she going to do with so many?

She told me that she grew her own vegetables and that not one slug was going to feed on them. I could not believe her attitude. What about all the deadly chemicals being absorbed by the vegetables as the slug pellets disintegrated?

If I grow anything, the slugs are quite welcome to a few bites. I'd rather have slugs than be poisoned through greed.

If more people studied organic gardening, then the use of chemicals would be minimal. I have not used any chemicals in my garden for six years. The previous owners had left boxes of slug pellets everywhere, and for the first two years there was very little wildlife in the garden. Now we see hedgehogs and unusual birds like goldfinches all the time. They know that it is a safe garden.

The Water Supply

This is getting worse all the time. Our water supply is contaminated by our rivers, and I do not believe that it is possible to extract or neutralize all the poisons that are deposited in the water. A substance that has been in water leaves the essence of itself behind.

Science thinks it has all the answers when trying to allay the fears of the general public, but people are not as easily duped as they used to be. Authority is now being questioned because we have been so let down by those in control. We must always be on the alert and insist that safety measures are carried out by qualified persons.

The seas around our shores are being poisoned every day. Chemicals are being released into the water in out of the way places that are very difficult to check. Fortunately, Greenpeace is always alert, and carries out dangerous and difficult assignments all the time. Everyone who is concerned about the environment their children will inherit should join an environmental group such as Greenpeace.

What about the companies who are releasing these chemicals and knowingly poisoning our rivers and seas? They do not care. To them it is just a question of making money and dumping the waste into someone else's backyard.

Nuclear waste, acid rain, polluted rivers and seas, illness caused by building on toxic waste ground, chemically polluted farmland that further pollutes the rivers – all can be attributed to greed. The cheapest way to dispose of straw and stubble is to burn it, adding to environmental contamination and the indiscriminate destruction of small wildlife, which are food for the predatory birds. The life-cycle is being broken down all the time.

Wildlife

The greed of ivory poachers is notorious. And yet it goes on, even though there has been a world-wide movement to stop this terrible practice. Baby elephants are left to die alongside their mutilated parents, and even if they are found in time to save them they still cry like babies for their mothers. Even the carers cannot bear the heart-break of these young animals.

Watching such beautiful creatures as baby seals being clubbed to death for their furs is one of the most diabolical scenes I have ever witnessed. Even on the television screen, the stark greed showed on the faces of their executioners. There can be no excuse for this kind of shocking behaviour.

Caught in the drag nets that stretch for miles across the ocean, dolphins die in the most horrendous way. These sensitive mammals are the most joyous of sea creatures and have shown great sensitivity to human beings who have been in danger of drowning. This is their reward.

Dr David Nathanson, a clinical psychologist working in Miami, has found that dolphins have a special relationship with handicapped children. Their healing qualities have enabled children to speak for the first time when all other help has failed.

They have been used and abused by humans for centuries. It is only now that we are beginning to realize that we can learn from them.

Despite repeated attempts to obtain international agreement to stop the slaughter of whales, which are wonderful, harmless creatures, some nations still try to find excuses, such as 'scientific research', to continue. Why don't they just admit to greed?

I have always been amazed that human beings can treat songbirds with such cruelty. But again greed rears its ugly head.

They are treated as a delicacy all over Europe. Can you imagine how little meat there is on a skylark or a robin? They are just feathers and bone. The beauty of their song should far outweigh the need to tempt anyone's taste buds.

Beautiful songbirds are trapped in tiny cages and sold, spending the rest of their lives in a living hell. Used to the freedom of the skies, these birds with their heart-breaking songs are held for ever behind bars simply to satisfy the whims of selfish and greedy people.

The people that catch parrots and export them all over the world do it only for greed. There are many beautiful species that have been lost to us for ever because of this inhumane trade. A large amount of the birds die *en route*, and those that survive are caged or, at the very best, cooped up in a room. Some owners try to teach these birds to talk, taking away their last shred of dignity. Can you imagine the agony of these birds? Their life should be in a warm climate, flying in groups from tree to tree. They are not by nature solitary creatures, and yet when they are caught that is what they are forced to be for the rest of their lives.

Many people are now trying to stop this terrible trade, but it has been going on for hundreds of years. How long will it take?

I could write a book about these tragedies, but by bringing these problems to your notice, I hope I am inspiring you to do your bit for the creatures of the world.

If human beings could curb their greed and bring some sanity into this world by doing their bit for the environment and for their fellow man, perhaps there is a chance of survival. But if it is left to governments who put off the issues until the year 2000, then I doubt if this planet can recover. It is in a far worse state than anyone would dare declare.

I do hope that *you* can help.

27

Fear

Fear is another totally destructive emotion. It is debilitating and takes away freedom of thought, word and deed.

Fear in Personal Relationships

This is the cause of many heart-breaking situations. If one half of the partnership is too afraid to discuss problems within that relationship, it can only lead to disaster. Make no mistake, sooner or later, the truth will become known no matter how good you are at hiding things.

Fear can reduce a human being to a cringing wreck in no time at all. This can be brought on by mental stress and cruelty given out most of the time by totally insensitive people – many of whom are so insensitive that they cannot understand the reactions to their behaviour. The situation becomes a vicious circle, as the victim grows more fearful of confrontation because they do not want their physical state to worsen.

There *is* a way to combat it, however, and that is to remove oneself from the presence of the person who is making you ill. This can be difficult however, especially where there are children and shared financial responsibilities.

It is possible, though, to be courageous – if you just take

one day at a time. Try to speak out about the little things that aggravate you, and do not allow yourself to be put down. There is no need to quarrel. Simply state the facts as you see them, and tell your partner that your opinions still stand even if they do not happen to agree with them. Once you have faced your fear, every day will be another challenge. Can you overcome the fear altogether? It is not possible to answer that question until you have given your new-found courage a chance. There will always be setbacks, and you will have to proceed with caution if you want the relationship to improve. If you don't, then that is another matter altogether.

No human being has the right to control another in this way. If it happens and the oppressor is allowed to get away with it, then the problem can become incurable.

Emotional Blackmail

Emotional blackmail is very common within a relationship. It has nothing at all to do with love, and should be stopped at the outset. The problem here is that when two people are supposedly in love, they are also trusting, so that it can take a hold without the other realizing what is happening. When it finally dawns on them, it can take an enormous amount of courage to put the situation right. Every case is unique, and everyone must find their own answers, but at all costs you must at least try. Otherwise you will never know how courageous you can be. The following story may help you.

A young woman came to me and asked for clairvoyance. I suggested that I gave her healing first, and then perhaps she would receive clairvoyance. She was hesitant at first, but I assured her that the healing was necessary.

Whilst I was giving her contact healing, she told me

about her husband. He was apparently obsessed with her. She said, 'I can't go anywhere alone. If I happen to slip out for a few minutes to visit my neighbour, it is only a short time before he is there also. He is making my life a misery.'

I asked her if there was any reason for him to feel insecure. She told me that he had been given all the assurances and all the love that he could possibly need. We talked about the problem at length, and it appeared that she had done everything in her power to cure it. At one time she had stayed at home for six months to try to prove to him that there was no-one else in her life. But this had not cured the problem.

It was quite obvious when I saw her that she was really in a very bad condition, both mentally and physically, and that was why I suggested healing. It had worked. Pouring out her problems to me obviously helped a little; storing them up inside can create further catastrophes.

Her husband had refused psychiatric help as he didn't think there was anything wrong with him. This is quite common. When someone is sick they are generally the last person to recognize the fact.

Her main worry was that he was now becoming violent. I suggested that she packed her cases and returned to her parents' home for the time being so that she could recover her own health.

She looked at me in silence for a very long time, and then she said, 'I am too frightened to leave. I know that he would follow me everywhere and might even cause me physical harm.'

I had heard these words only too often, and knew that I had to persuade her to seek some sort of sanctuary. Clairvoyantly, I could tell that she was in danger.

She left promising me that she would think about it.

The next time I saw her she was covered in bruises and crying so much that it was difficult to talk, but she made it clear that no matter how frightened she was she was going to leave her husband.

This did not happen for four months. In that time she was repeatedly abused mentally and physically.

She eventually found the courage to go back to her parents, and when she visited me next told me that her husband had proved to be too cowardly to carry out his threats of violence. She said, 'If only I had listened to you in the first place I would not have had to go through all this misery.' I asked her what had given her the courage to leave in the end. She told me that she had asked for help out loud, and when she woke in the morning all fear had gone.

Her statement did not surprise me in the least. I have been told many times by patients that praying silently hadn't brought any results, but when they made their request out loud it had been answered. I have experienced this myself. Perhaps we should all make our presence felt in this way more often.

Criticism

Criticism also creates a situation of fear within a relationship. It can reduce one partner to a shaking wreck, afraid to voice their opinions for fear of being put down, especially in company.

It is a question, once more, of finding the courage to walk away. There is no point in arguing with someone who behaves in such a domineering way. Constructive criticism can be beneficial, but even that can be taken too far if the recipient finds it difficult to handle.

Cowards

Cowardly people are always living in fear, blaming others for their faults because they just cannot face reality. It is very difficult for cowards to change; such behaviour is usually an inherent part of their personality.

There are very few people who are not afraid of physical violence. This is normal. One may appear to be a coward when violence is lurking, but this is only self-preservation, not the type of cowardice I am referring to.

I have seen some very nice people turn into a Jekyll and Hyde type of character simply because they were too afraid to own up to a misdeed. Rather than face the music, they have brought innocent people into the charade and allowed it to reach dangerous proportions. It is very difficult to understand how they live with their own conscience; cowardice and lies are bedfellows.

There are certain people who simply put their head in the sand and refuse to believe that a situation is developing until it has got out of hand. When this moment arrives they convince themselves that it has nothing whatever to do with them.

Illness

Fear is a major problem with illness. Simply having hospital tests can start the heart hammering, which in turn causes breathing problems.

When the specialist assures you that there is nothing wrong, it is sometimes difficult to comprehend. The imagination has already gone overboard, and can take some time to calm down.

When the diagnosis is bad, fear can take a heavy toll, and can actually cause further symptoms which prevent alleviation of the original disease.

One reaches the lowest point at night. This is the time when fear takes over completely.

There are many ways of overcoming fear in illness. You will find these in *Mind Magic*. I have seen some miraculous cures brought about through self-help, so whatever you do, never give up.

Bullies

Bullying at school has been going on for ever and I expect it always will. If one child is weak and frightened, it brings out the bully in another child.

Teachers have to be on their guard against this all the time, but bullies can be crafty, turning on the charm whenever necessary. That is why it can be very difficult to confront them. Their parents, of course, would never admit to their child being a bully, even when the evidence is damning.

I have known children who have been absolutely petrified of going to school because they are being bullied. Bullies being cowards, tend to surround themselves with friends of similar nature and appear even more menacing. Their frightened victims are often subjected to the most harrowing indignities.

Fear has forced children to hand over their dinner money. Their parents believe they are having a decent meal when, in fact, they are extremely hungry and can become undernourished.

Bullying children left unpunished grow up to be bullying adults. To prevent them growing up like this, they must be confronted and punished whilst they are still at an impressionable age. On no account should they be allowed to get away with this most horrible trait.

Parents who turn a blind eye are not helping their

children at all as, at some stage in their lives, they will be recognized for what they are, and they will be shunned by all decent people.

Do not allow fear to become a part of your life. Treat yourself to a new life of freedom of thought, word and deed.

28

Joy

Joy! What an incredible feeling it is, and one that we ought to seek all the time. Alas, it is so lacking in today's society.

When we are young we are joyful most of the time unless there are particular negative or sad influences around, but as we grow up and have to face responsibilities, the joy gradually disappears.

Of course, there are many occasions in life when joy returns, and it is then that we realize what we are missing and hope that we can retain these moments. There *is* a way, but it involves putting others before yourself.

I believe that there can be no greater joy than to help others. Perhaps you could sit and listen, allowing someone to unburden themselves of their worries and anxieties. This is a great healer in itself.

If you have an hour to spare once a week to give a housebound person an outing or take them shopping, this will increase your own happiness as well as theirs. Perhaps you are a gardener, and can help in this way.

Neighbours can help one another when they are ill, simply by shopping for those small necessary items. If you have a telephone, why not have a conversation once a week with someone who is bedridden? This takes up very little time and gives so much pleasure.

Joy is a feeling that comes from the heart. If your motives are wrong, this emotion will be absent.

Pure joy is ecstasy and it is very rare. When it happens, you will feel as though you are walking on air. Your mind and body will be in harmony, and you will forget the material world.

Material things have nothing to do with this state, which is an experience of the soul. You are simply receiving what you have given.

Selfish people never experience joy, because their happiness is always subconsciously tinged with guilt. This does not prevent them from seeking it, and they will try to do so by acquiring many possessions. Unfortunately, their search will be fruitless because they will never find what they are looking for until they no longer need to possess.

I have seen so many lives deteriorate in this way. Some people were lucky enough to have seen the light, and so have simplified their lives. This usually brings them into contact with more caring people, which in turn has brought them peace and happiness such as they had never known.

Our mind is our greatest possession. Every now and then it needs a spring clean, but otherwise it serves us extremely well.

Why not spring clean your mind now, and bring back the joy in your life?

PART SEVEN

THE CHILD

29

The Child Within

To be happy, one can never afford to lose the child within. A child is innocent and has faith, and allows things to happen. It has no critical faculty, and the negative thoughts that close the mind do not exist.

A child has not yet let go of the energy dimension from whence it came. It cries for the beauty and the silence that it has lost by electing to return to this gross materialistic world, and it sheds tears for those unhappy people who spend their lives trying to shatter dreams by forcing others to face *their* reality.

Reality? These people have no idea what that is. The world the child has left is reality. This planet is the dream-state, the nightmare that one cannot escape until it is time for us to awake.

As the child grows, it has to be taught how to survive – the human way; their instinctive knowledge of survival is suppressed.

There is nothing as spontaneous as a child's laughter. So many adults have forgotten how to laugh.

Children believe in fairies, gnomes, goblins and Father Christmas. Older children, who are gradually losing their reality, do not hesitate in trying to take their beliefs away from them. Their own lives have been spoilt by being plunged into this material world too early, and they resent having lost the child within. Their magic having been torn

261

from them, they cease to believe in themselves and lose confidence.

They do not know what they can achieve. Ask them to reach for the stars, and they laugh. They do not understand that stardom is in each and every one of us. We simply have to know, without doubt, that it is there.

We are all born with talent, and it takes the child within to find and nurture it.

The kind of stardom that I am writing about is not that of show business, but in the achievements of the soul, of finding ourselves and being committed to truth and one's destiny.

There are millions of people all over the world who have lost the child within because they have suffered poverty, disease or violence. Let those of us who have been able to retain it help them with our love, energy and commitment.

Let us also open the eyes of those near to us, so that they can understand and appreciate the *true* reality and bring back the child within them – to allow things to happen.

Above all, help them to understand that minds from other dimensions are waiting to help. To be able to listen to audible silence and receive telepathic messages for ourselves is the ultimate achievement.

To be able to glimpse reality only once in a lifetime is enough – it is never forgotten. Once you have this key, you have the key to the child within. Don't ever lose it.

30

For the Children of the World

There has been a message running through my three books, *Mind to Mind*, *Mind Magic* and now *Mind Waves* – that human beings have a lot to learn.

Our greatest gift is the mind, and the mind is an energy that spans all dimensions. I have tried to teach you how to use every atom of that power, not only to reach your potential, but to go beyond, to break down the barriers that have been constructed over the centuries by misguided and ignorant people, to grow spiritually so that a pure love enters your life which enables you to share your experiences.

Healing each other and sending healing thoughts around the world is only the beginning, but it *is* a beginning. There are thousands of non-starters that we have to carry, and they can be a heavy burden. Nevertheless, there can be no turning back.

This planet is a sick place, and we are all responsible for that in one way or another. Thoughts that are collectively bound together with hate, vindictiveness, greed, selfishness, jealousy and other negative emotions, are power.

There have been and still are misguided scientists who have placed the whole world at risk. And there have also been scientists who have discovered life-saving treatments. Unfortunately, we always have to take the bad with the good.

An article in *The Mail on Sunday*, 17 November 1991, told of millions of tons of radioactive waste which is scattered near Germany's frontier with Czechoslovakia, over an area the size of Bedfordshire. Mountains of toxic rocks mark the sites of uranium mines that once fuelled the arms race. Thousands of tons of this rubble have been used in the construction of roads, houses, schools and railways throughout Germany. Water supplies are contaminated, and so is the dust carried on the wind which the children are inhaling. The air, the earth, and the milk they drink are all potential killers.

The cancer wards of hospitals in south-east Germany are filled with young children dying from leukaemia. One of the children said, 'There is a green dragon living on this hill that is eating us all up.'

This particular time bomb will stay lethal for 800,000 years. This is the legacy these children have inherited, and if they live long enough it will affect their own children and their offspring.

Psychics have forecast these disasters for centuries, and some scientists have had a field day at their expense. Now it can be seen that they were right to have such fears and forebodings. There are disasters all around us.

The children of our world will need all their awareness and psychic abilities to handle this legacy of destruction. They will have to learn clairvoyance – which after all is only clear vision – to be able to make the right decisions. Healing abilities will be needed in abundance.

But most of all, their mediumistic abilities will have to be finely tuned, so that they may receive help and advice from progressed minds.

The children that have these gifts in excess will be the true leaders of the world. It is a parent's duty to help them to achieve these goals now – it is already too late to save a great proportion of our heritage, but we must do what we can *now* to try to balance the scales.

The water in our own country is becoming more polluted; in some areas people have even been poisoned by the accidental addition of chemicals. In future we will all be well advised to drink spring water from bottles – in fact a great many people are already doing so.

There are sites all over the nation where toxic matter has been dumped. No records of these dumps have been kept, so no-one knows where they are. People living in houses that have been built on these sites have been sick ever since they moved in. Residents from a whole estate were given alternative living accommodation when the roads and grass around the estate were found to be radioactive. Tenants who were questioned admitted that both they and their children had been sick whilst they had lived on the estate. Why were these houses built on a site that was known to be unsafe?

I have been told of another site, near a village, which has had toxic waste dumped on it for years. It was eventually covered up and left. Two years ago, lorries carrying waste from the site were seen trundling down the village high street twelve hours a day. These lorries were covered with metal sheets and the roads were washed down after they had passed. The villagers were terrified. They realized that they were in danger, but nobody could find out what was behind this sudden removal of toxic waste. Months later, they saw houses being built on the site. Still more unsuspecting people will come from afar to take possession of these houses, unaware of the dangers. And so the sickness will continue until someone in authority has the courage to do something about it.

We are told by governments that reductions will be made to the level of pollution by the year 2000. What they do not understand is that it is already too late to recover what we have lost. Something drastic has to be done *now* for our children. Let us forget ourselves and think of them. They are the future, they will be coping with this planet when we are all dead. Let us try to leave them a purer environment.

We must help them to become aware, to know the secrets of other dimensions and to know that they can ask for help from these dimensions.

If the parents read my books and practise the teachings themselves, they can teach their children. The secrets are there on every page.

Do this now in your own home, and for all the children of the world. It is so simple.

Live by Universal Law. It is the finest and fairest judgement of all.

PART EIGHT

STRANGE HAPPENINGS

31

Strange Happenings

In addition to the stories that you have already read in this book, other very strange things have been happening to me since I wrote *Mind Magic*.

In June 1990 I decided to have two weeks holiday in Spain. I had been overworking for many years, and this was taking its toll. I was suffering from recurring symptoms that were making my life very uncomfortable, and one night, just before going to sleep, I looked at the ceiling and said, 'If you want me to carry on with this work, do something.'

Of course, I had already treated my problems with mind exercises and vitamins and minerals, and had I gone on doing so, this would, no doubt, have brought about a cure in the end. But I am extremely impatient with myself, hence the threat.

When I woke in the morning I accidentally touched my body on the left side just below the heart. It was extremely painful. When I investigated I found a red scar the length of my forefinger with seventeen stitch marks. And round the scar were what looked like seventeen clamp marks. I stared in disbelief.

Over the years my patients have reported the manifestation of scars after I had performed psychic operations on them – but not, to my knowledge, with stitch and clamp marks. I had been sleeping alone in my room covered only by a sheet because of the heat. No-one had been anywhere near me.

Obviously, I could not show my scar to everyone but my family certainly saw it.

My recurring symptoms disappeared completely, but the scar was still faintly visible six months later.

Whenever I have threatened whoever may be listening in the spirit world with giving up my work, it seems to have produced results. Perhaps there are times when we have to become very angry in order for our mind energy to expand enough to penetrate other dimensions. Anger is a very positive thing.

In 1991 I was invited to visit some crop circles – in Wiltshire, where most of them seem to occur. I took my tape recorder with me as, over the years, many strange noises have been taped whilst I was giving healing. I wondered whether there might be any unusual energy in the circles, and if so, whether it could be healing energy. Many of those who have studied the crop circles believe them to have a healing connection. I had no preconceived ideas on the nature of these circles; I had a completely open mind.

I had travelled with friends, and when we were nearing our destination, we saw a most beautiful crop circle formation which had appeared the previous night. It was in an inaccessible position, but as it was carved out of the wheat on the slope of a steep hill, it could easily be seen from the road. To our surprise, other new circles had also appeared in the same vicinity.

The first two circles we entered were extremely interesting, one small new one having been formed overnight beside an old one. It was almost as though it had given birth. However, because the circle was so new there were a lot of other visitors about, so we didn't stay long.

We then made our way to some circles which had been formed the previous week. Leaving the car, we waded through the wheat and eventually sat down in one of the circles. I put the tape recorder down beside me and switched it on. My friends did the same with their own recorders. I closed my eyes and relaxed.

I had a feeling of absolute peace and harmony, and had a vision of lights, almost like searchlights, being beamed down on to the ground. I do not know whether these lights had anything to do with the formation of the circle.

Ten minutes later, I rewound the tape and played it back. The noise it produced was unbelievable, rather like the hammering of a road drill. My friends had nothing at all on their recorders, and thought mine must be faulty. One of them asked if she could record on my machine, and I agreed, but suggested that as I was a medium it should be placed by my side. This she did. When she played it back five minutes later, it produced the same noise, which we had by now nicknamed the woodpecker – admittedly rather a loud one. It was then suggested that the three tape recorders should be placed in a pile to see if the sound could be transferred. This time none of the recorders had any sound on them.

The tape recorder I had used was practically new, so I was almost certain that there was nothing wrong with it. But I was prepared to keep an open mind on the subject.

For years I have recorded my healing sessions, as the energy produces a sound like rushing water and this fascinates my patients. A week after visiting the crop circles, I put a new tape into my recorder during a healing session. When I played it back, there was the woodpecker hammering away. Thinking now that the machine was indeed faulty, I decided to record without actually doing any contact healing. I played the tape back a few minutes later and the woodpecker had gone, leaving only the normal healing energy sound. I suggested to my patient that I did a further five minutes contact healing, which I recorded. The woodpecker returned.

I decided to speak into the recorder, simply saying, 'I am not healing now,' because I felt there was an intelligence involved. On replay, the woodpecker had gone. Then I spoke into the recorder and said, 'I am now healing.' It returned. My patient and I were so fascinated that we continued in this fashion for over two hours. At one time I tried to trick it by saying that I was healing, when I wasn't. But there was no response from the woodpecker, proving there really was an intelligence behind it.

Someone suggested that, when I was in healing mode, I was linking up with a powerful source of energy in this dimension. But as the hammering started before I had finished my sentence, there was obviously a clairvoyant factor at work.

The woodpecker is never recorded whilst I am healing my family. Neither will it perform when I sit alone. It only appears when I have patients.

I was invited to a party given by a close friend. Whilst I was at his home, quite by chance I sat about five feet away from his tape recorder. It has two recording units, one of which only takes metallic tapes. The next morning, his cleaner accidentally knocked the metallic tape switch – and there was the woodpecker. My friend had heard the noise during a healing session, so he recognized it immediately. The strangest thing is that there was no tape in the machine. Where was the sound coming from? It is still there to this day, and he cannot use that part of his recorder.

A similar thing happened with the recorder of another

friend, but she lost the noise after a week or so.

Who or what is this mysterious woodpecker? I have no doubt at all that it is an intelligence, but what is it trying to tell me?

It is obviously from another dimension, and this was proved when two patients came to me for healing one hot summer's day. The one who wasn't receiving healing sat in the garden under the shade of a tree. I left the french windows of my healing room open to let in the breeze.

I switched on the tape recorder. All was peaceful. Suddenly, there was an incredibly loud noise outside. Looking out of the window, I saw a police helicopter circling the area at roof-top height. The friend who was in the garden ran into the healing room, frightened to death. The helicopter continued to circle for a long time; we couldn't talk – our words were drowned by the noise.

Later, when I had finished healing both of them, I played back the recorder. I had actually forgotten that it had been recording, and I assumed that all we would hear would be the helicopter. We were all amazed, however, when we heard the woodpecker, which had completely blotted out the din from outside. That is why I know that this phenomenon is from another dimension.

Using the tape recorder in the crop circle has started a series of different phenomena. I never know from one day to the next what surprises it has in store for me.

On one occasion, I used a new tape – I took it out of its cellophane wrapper myself – to record whilst healing. When I played it back, I found that I was listening to a conversation that I had had with a journalist three months previously. The only recorder in the room at the time had belonged to the interviewer.

About a week after this, I was having lunch when a voice said that I should go and sit in the healing room with my husband and make a recording. When I told Alan this, he downed tools and sat in the room with me. Again, a new tape was used. By this time I was spending a fortune on tapes.

We sat quietly for about half an hour, and then I was told to switch the recorder off. When we played the tape back, it produced a conversation between the two of us that had taken place a fortnight previously, in the office. I have never used the recorder in the office – and it *was* a brand new tape.

We have also heard someone playing the violin. It was very beautiful and totally unexpected.

Something very odd is also happening with my computer. Twice, when I have been trying to remember the date – month and year – of stories I wanted to use in this book, the information, without any warning, has come up on the computer screen. On both occasions it was correct. Perhaps it is my subconscious that is activating the computer. The mind is certainly a magical energy.

One day, I was listening to the messages on my answerphone. One was from a journalist on a well-known magazine, asking me to ring a particular number so that she could speak to me. I returned her call but could not remember her name, so just said that someone wished to speak to me for an article in the magazine.

The person who answered the phone tried to trace the caller, but with no success, so I was then put through to the editor. She hadn't called me either. After I had replaced the phone, I listened to the taped message again. It was quite long and very clear, and this time I wrote the name of the caller on a piece of paper.

I phoned again, and asked for the journalist by name. It happened to belong to the woman who had answered my first call – and she was also the person who was writing the article – but she said she hadn't called me. When I asked her if she would like to listen to her own voice, her amazement was quite genuine. Putting the phone to the answering machine I switched on her message. When it had finished, she exclaimed, 'I can't believe it. It's my voice and my way of speaking, but I swear to you that I did not make that call.'

I contacted her again the next day as I still could not believe that she hadn't made the call. She remained adamant. In fact she told me that she had checked her diary, as every name had to be recorded there when a call had been made and a return call was expected. My name was not in the book, and no-one in the office could shed any light on the mystery.

I believe that whilst she was writing the piece about me, she may have thought of ringing me for confirmation, then changed her mind, and the thought had been transferred to my machine by mind waves. It is the only possible explanation I can give.

On another occasion, I was healing the wife of a man in his late seventies. He had carried out tests on healers for many years and was very interested in everything concerned with healing waves.

I switched on the tape recorder so that he could hear the woodpecker if it came through during the session. He fell asleep whilst I was healing his wife; this is not unusual as the healing room fills with energy. His wife, on the other hand, was very much awake, and we carried on a conversation throughout the healing.

When I had finished, I played the tape back. It was quite incredible. The conversation that his wife and I had throughout the healing was not recorded. Instead, we were listening to the voice of the sleeping man – his thoughts had been recorded. He, of course, had not been aware of any thought process whilst he was asleep, but he told me that what had been recorded was what he had been thinking about all week.

It has long been my wish to record spirit voices. After these experiences, I am sure that it is possible to do this. After all, no matter what dimension one is in, there is still a mind-to-mind link.

It is quite unbelievable how many strange things have happened – all of them unexpected. I have asked many times for specific gifts, but most of my requests are ignored and something quite different is given.

On a more humorous note, there was a hornbeam tree in our garden, approximately fifty feet high. It overshadowed the flower beds, and the shrubs near this tree were in bad condition because of the lack of sunlight. My husband and I applied for permission to take the top out of the tree, but this was refused as it had a preservation order on it.

I was so annoyed that I said I would ask for a gale to blow it down. That was the first week of October 1987. Two weeks later, the centre of the tree, which is the only piece we wanted removed, was blown down during the night of the famous hurricane which destroyed fifteen million trees. It fell just short of the house, only damaging some guttering – it was that close. Alan said afterwards, 'You shouldn't have gone to those lengths to get rid of that tree.' I know he is sometimes amazed at my powers, but this was ridiculous.

So many strange things happen to me. A few could be put down to coincidence, but who knows? Life would certainly be very dull if they all stopped. I certainly hope they don't.

Summing up

Throughout the whole of this book I have tried to show you how mind waves invade everything around us. I have given you the evidence, and now you, the reader, can begin your own voyage of discovery with the simple exercises in this book.

What other explanation can cover the whole of the paranormal?

My discovery and subsequent study of mind energy and waves has opened up new dimensions for myself and thousands of people around the world. The impact of it all is still to come.

The realization that we leave behind memories and the quality of our minds in inanimate objects as well as in the ether must, at some time, alter the way we think.

Universal Law is absolute. This applies to other universes as well as our own. Nobody knows all the secrets of the Universe. We can only guess, but most certainly there are people contacting us all the time through survival evidence and by the other means mentioned in this book.

At some time, everyone will have to take off their blinkers and recognize evidence that will not go away.

Over the years mediums have received hundreds of warnings from spirits about the ecology. We have been warned, but as usual if something cannot be seen, it will be ignored. Now we can see, but those in control *still* ignore the signs. It is left to a small band of courageous people to fight these issues.

The more arduous investigations must be carried out by the young and active, but there is a role for everyone on this planet, and it is up to every single one of us to find our particular role and carry it through.

There is no need to become obsessional and lose our friends in the process. The majority of such work is done by quiet, calm, individuals.

We would all feel happier, healthier and more peaceful knowing that every day in some way we had offered a helping hand to someone in need. You do not need to be a do-gooder, or to be a saint. Simply be yourself.

I have never been a saint, and I am sure I will never achieve that status in any dimension – I am too much of a rebel – but I do try to achieve something different every day. I love to challenge my own mind potential.

Challenge! That is the word that has inspired me throughout my life. Why don't you take up the challenge of helping to make this world a better place to live in?

Bibliography

Benham, William G., *Laws of Scientific Hand Reading*, Tarporevala, Bombay, 1975

Bhaktivendanta, Swami Prabhupada, *Bhagavad Gita*, Bhaktivendanta Book Trust, London and Sydney, 1968

Davies, Dr Stephen and Stewart, Dr Alan, *Nutritional Medicine*, Pan Books, London and Sydney, 1987

Deshpande, P. Y., *The Authentic Yoga*, Rider & Company, London, 1982

Erdmann, Dr Robert and Jones, Meiron, *The Amino Revolution*, Century Publishing Company, London, 1987

Garde, Dr R. K. *Yoga Therapy*, Wolfe, New Delhi, 1973

Harris, Bertha, *Traveller in Eternity*, Regency Press, London and New York, 1956, reprinted in 1975

Harrison, Peter and Mary, *Life Before Birth*, Futura Macdonald & Co., London and Sydney, 1983

Hittleman, Richard, *Guide to Yoga Meditation*, Bantam Books, London, New York, Toronto, 1969

Hoyle, Fred and Wickramasinghe, N. C., *Diseases From Space*, Sphere Books, London, 1979

Iyengar, B. K. S., *Light on Yoga*, Allen & Unwin, London, 1968

Jaquin, Noel, *The Hand Speaks*, Sagar Publications, New Delhi, 1973

Meek, George W. and Harris, Bertha, *Seance To Science*, Regency Press, London and New York, 1973

Ouseley, S. G. J., *The Power of the Rays: The Science of*

Colour Healing, L. N. Fowler & Co. Ltd, London, 1975

Reiker, Hans-Ulrich, *The Yoga of Light*, The Dawn Horse Press, California, 1976

Schul, Bill, *The Psychic Power of Animals*, Coronet Books, London, 1977

Wolff, Charlotte, *The Hand In Psychological Diagnosis*, Sagar Publications, New Delhi, 1972

Finding a Medium

Appointments can be made with mediums at the following
  organizations:
The College of Psychic Studies, 16 Queensberry Place,
  London SW7 2EB. Tel. 071 589 3292
The Spiritualist Association of Great Britain, 33 Belgrave
  Square, London SW1 8QB. Tel. 071 235 3351

Finding a Healer

Please write to:

National Federation of Spiritual Healers,
Old Manor Farm Studio,
Church Street,
Sunbury-on-Thames
TW16 6RG.
Tel. 0932 783164

If you wish to write to me for absent healing and advice, please keep your letters brief.

I have recorded many tapes for self-healing and peace of mind. My daughter, Janet, has recorded mantras. These tapes, together with books and other self-help items, are available from the address below.

Betty Shine
PO Box 1009
Hassocks
West Sussex
BN6 8XS

S.A.E. essential!

MIND TO MIND
by Betty Shine

Betty Shine is a remarkable woman. Her extraordinary gifts – a clairvoyant ability to diagnose medically, her healing powers and her discovery of 'mind energy' – have made her one of Britain's foremost healers.

Mind to Mind tells her story. Like Betty herself, it is cheerful, down-to-earth and full of humour. It reveals how she became aware of her gifts and how she has used her experiences of mind energy to help others. Illustrated with a wide variety of examples and case histories, this is a uniquely helpful and practical book by a woman whose powers have been a comfort and an inspiration to countless numbers of people.

'It is a positive, optimistic book, which I am sure will be a great encouragement to anyone who believes that the mind is capable of much more than we can presently dream of'
Michael Aspel

'This is a rare book, written by a rare person. I know that you will enjoy reading it'
Michael Bentine

'Full of fascinating case histories'
Guardian

'Fascinating and very readable . . . compelling and informative . . . written with humility and intelligence'
Psychic News

0 552 13378 7

MIND MAGIC
by Betty Shine

Since her first book, *Mind to Mind*, was published in 1989, Betty Shine has been inundated with letters of thanks and appreciation. Her extraordinary message has touched hearts and changed lives the world over. As her reputation has grown, it has become impossible for Betty to treat personally the thousands of people who look to her for help. So it is as a natural extension of her talks, lectures and private consultations that she has written *Mind Magic*, a self-help guide that will enable everyone to experience the benefits of mind energy and healing – for themselves and for the good of others.

At the core of *Mind Magic* is a series of exercises and projects devised, tried and tested by Betty herself. Though all have been designed to develop the imagination and renew mind energy, each has an additional specific aim, ranging from stress management to memory enhancement. Built around these disciplines is a mass of practical advice on vitamin and mineral intake, colour therapy, the power of positive thinking and a host of other topics. A handbook for the soul, a guide to health and happiness, a manual for living in the modern world, *Mind Magic* is a valuable and singular contribution to New Age literature.

'I am quite convinced that she has certain remarkable powers'
Val Hennessy, *Mail on Sunday*

'Clearly written and lively . . . thoroughly recommended'
Psychic News

0 552 13671 9

BETTY SHINE'S MIND WORKBOOK
Exercises linking mind, body and spirit
by Betty Shine

The essential guide to self-knowledge.

Betty Shine's three extraordinary bestsellers, *Mind to Mind*, *Mind Magic* and *Mind Waves* have inspired countless readers all over the world. Her gifts as a psychic healer, her study of mind energy and the benefits its use can bring, and her personal warmth, charisma and vitality have caused her to be acclaimed on all sides by her devoted and ever-growing public.

Betty Shine's Mind Workbook provides simple exercises which even the busiest lifestyle can accommodate. Recognizing the need for a workbook which combined mind exercises selected from Betty's earlier books and also offered new examples, this is a complete manual, enhanced by poetry and prose quotations, for living healthily and happily in today's world. Pages are supplied for the reader to record observations, emotions, and progress – as Betty says, 'This book will represent the real you, and I know you will be surprised at what you will find out about yourself.'

0 552 14214 X

A SELECTION OF RELATED TITLES
AVAILABLE FROM CORGI BOOKS

☐ 14144 5   **POSSESSED**   *Thomas B. Allen* £4.99

☐ 13653 0   **THE RELUCTANT JESTER**   *Michael Bentine* £5.99

☐ 09828 0   **THE PROPHECIES OF NOSTRADAMUS**   *Erika Cheetham* £4.99

☐ 12299 8   **THE FURTHER PROPHECIES OF NOSTRADAMUS**   *Erika Cheetham* £3.50

☐ 11487 1   **LIFE AFTER DEATH**   *Neville Randall* £3.99

☐ 14214 X   **BETTY SHINE'S MIND WORKBOOK**   *Betty Shine* £6.99

☐ 13378 7   **MIND TO MIND**   *Betty Shine* £4.99

☐ 13671 9   **MIND MAGIC**   *Betty Shine* £4.99